ScriptureWalk Junior High
Bible Themes

ScriptureWalk Junior High
Bible Themes

Bible-Based Sessions for Teens

Maryann Hakowski

Saint Mary's Press
Christian Brothers Publications
Winona, Minnesota

To the teens of
Holy Spirit Parish, Virginia Beach, Virginia,
and
Saint Nicholas Church, O'Fallon, Illinois,
who dared to bring the Scriptures to Life

Genuine recycled paper with 10% post-consumer waste.
Printed with soy-based ink.

The publishing team included Brian Singer-Towns, development editor; Mary Duerson, copy editor; Barbara Bartelson, production editor; Hollace Storkel, typesetter; Stephan Nagel, art director; Alicia María Sánchez, cover designer; pre-press, printing, and binding by the graphics division of Saint Mary's Press.

The acknowledgments continue on page 104.

Printed in the United States of America

Printing: 9 8 7 6 5 4 3 2 1

Year: 2007 06 05 04 03 02 01 00 99

ISBN 0-88489-607-2

Contents

Introduction

The Reason for the ScriptureWalk Series

The Bible is one of the best-selling books of all time, yet so many copies sit on the shelf collecting dust. Why is this? Perhaps because so many people misunderstand the Bible's purpose. It is more than a dictionary or encyclopedia of faith. It is more than good storytelling or a collection of historical trivia. It is not "just an old book written by a bunch of old guys," as one teen told me!

Vatican Council II opened the doors for Catholics to read and study the Bible with renewed fervor. In the last few decades, parish Scripture study groups have sprung up across the country as Catholic adults began to enthusiastically explore the Bible. However, the Catholic scriptural renewal has yet to fully flower among Catholic young people, partly owing to a lack of resources designed to engage Catholic young people in Bible study and reflection. The ScriptureWalk series is designed to help fill that gap.

Bringing the Scriptures to Life

God speaks to us through the Bible whomever we are and wherever we are and whatever age we might be. The Bible is a source of strength and a source of challenge. The Scriptures have an incredible power to transform our life. If we invite the Scriptures off the written page and into our life and heart, we cannot help but be changed in a radical way. The *ScriptureWalk Junior High* sessions in this book will help you in making the Bible come alive for your junior high youth.

The Bible and Evangelization

When we make the Bible come alive, it is one of our primary sources of evangelization. Let's look at some of the principles of evangelization and how they help us understand how to use the Bible with young people.

Evangelization is dynamic. We cannot just hand a Bible to young people and say, "Here, read this." We must approach the Scriptures with a sense of enthusiasm and anticipation and fun so that the young people will too.

Evangelization occurs through relationships. We need to spend time with young people so that we can understand how their experiences connect with the teachings of the Bible.

Evangelization takes place where people are. We need to take the Bibles beyond the classroom and the church library and into the school lockers and gym bags and rooms at home and ball fields and fast-food restaurants, because these are the places where the Bible must be lived to make sense to our young people today.

Evangelization takes time. Reading the Bible takes practice. Loving the Bible takes a lifetime. We want young people to get into the habit of spending time with the Bible. Only then can they begin to proclaim the Scriptures with their life.

The Origins of These Sessions

The eight sessions in this book were originally designed for the junior high youth group at Holy Spirit Parish in Virginia Beach, Virginia, where I served as pastoral associate for three years. We already had a vibrant senior high youth group. A team of teens planned and facilitated the meetings around themes of interest to youth. I encouraged them to include the Scriptures whenever possible.

To meet the needs of our junior high young people, we decided to start a junior high youth group. We took a decidedly different approach by starting with the Scriptures, and then making the connection to the lives of the young people.

While some parents expressed doubts that a Scripture-based program would appeal to the young people, we felt that the active-learning approach was the key to our success. Our young people had a yearning for the Gospels, which surprised and moved us. We met once a month, on a Monday night, but at the time I left the parish, both parents and young people were calling for more frequent meetings, at least twice a month.

The Goals of *ScriptureWalk Junior High: Bible Themes*

ScriptureWalk Junior High: Bible Themes has four goals:

- That the sessions invite the young people to "break open" the Scriptures
- That the activities are fun and engaging
- That the sessions experiment with a variety of prayer forms
- That each meeting differs from the one before it

The Structure of *ScriptureWalk Junior High*

The *ScriptureWalk Junior High* manuals are structured on the principle of active learning. Each 90-minute session includes activities to build community, engage young people in discussion, and introduce them to creative forms of prayer. A discussion of the principle of active learning and the activities that flow from it follows.

Active Learning

We retain only a small percentage of what we see and hear, but when we experience something, when we engage all the senses and the entire person, we learn and remember so much more.

Young adolescents are not the "sit still and learn" types. In fact they are not "sit still" types at all. They have a lot of energy to burn and need constructive outlets for harnessing it. The variety of activities found in this book promote an active-learning model. When we use active-learning methods, rather than telling young people what they have learned, we ask them what they learned from an activity they just completed.

Community-Building Activities

Community-building activities, such as games or icebreakers, are opportunities for the young people to learn names, to stretch, and to be introduced to a session theme. For example, in session 7, "The Spirit's Promise," the young people hunt for clues to learn more about the Holy Spirit. In session 8, "Coming Home," a deck of cards is used as a vehicle to mix the group and start a discussion on forgiveness.

In the community-building activities, it is important to include everyone. Pay attention to two key tasks: (1) giving clear directions and (2) following up the activity with a group discussion or a short interactive presentation that enables the young people to discover what they have learned.

Dynamic Discussions

Leading dynamic discussions is an important part of active learning. You will find that discussion flows naturally from the thought-provoking activities in the sessions. For example, in session 4, "Being Thankful," the participants go from *A* to *Z* listing the many blessings God has given, which leads into a discussion on being thankful. In session 3, "Journey," they navigate a real obstacle course, then discuss how God can help them navigate the obstacles in their life.

Some of the discussions are designed for pairs, others for small or large groups. The discussion activities usually offer specific, open-ended questions so that the young people are encouraged to answer with more than one-word responses. Discussion gets easier as your group members meet more frequently and become more comfortable sharing with one another. If your group members need more time to adjust to sharing, offer to let them write down their answers before sharing.

As a general rule, try to assign people to small groups for discussion rather than let them choose their own groups. When asked to find their own groups, they tend to remain in cliques, making it harder to build community. Sharing in pairs may be more appropriate the first few times you gather, and then you can ease them into group discussions.

Powerful Prayer Services

By exposing young people to a variety of prayer experiences, we expand their personal repertoire of ways to approach God. Some forms of prayer found in this book include guided meditation, symbols, music, storytelling, video, quiet prayer, shared prayer, and traditional prayer.

The prayer experiences often use objects to appeal to the young peoples' concrete imaginations. For example, in the session 1 activity "The Lord Is My Light and My Salvation," the young people use flashlights to bring light into their prayer. In the session 2 activity "Praying with Change," they use coins to pray about their use of God's gifts.

Pay particular attention to the setting for prayer. If possible have a separate space away from your regular meeting space for other activities.

Scripture Connections

Each session uses several Scripture passages to offer insight into the session theme. These Scripture passages are given at the beginning of most activities. Generally directions for reading a passage or passages are given within the activity. Sometimes a passage is adapted or paraphrased for some use within an activity. And occasionally the passage simply provides a scriptural connection for the activity that is not explicitly mentioned. For further reflection additional Scripture passages relating to the theme are included at the end of each session.

Family Connection

Each session includes a section at the end called "Family Connection." It gives a short, family-based follow-up idea for the session. Some of the activities include affirmation, prayer, discussion, and community service. You may wish to share these ideas in a parent meeting, send them home in a newsletter, photocopy them for the participants, or simply suggest them to the young people at the end of a session.

Optional Activities

Each session also includes an optional activity that can be used in several ways:

- as a substitute for a session activity
- as a way to make the session longer
- as a follow-up activity

Look over this optional activity in advance to see if it fits your needs.

Suggestions for Program Leaders

A Bible for Every Teen

At the first session, make sure everyone in your youth group or class has a Bible. Don't just assume that they already own one. There is a good chance they do not. Having a few Bibles to share every time your group meets is not good enough. If we want young people to spend time with the Bible and make it part of their life, they must each have their own. We want their Bible to look worn and dog-eared. That will mean that it is being read and is traveling with the young people throughout their day and week and not just being dusted off now and then.

Use a Catholic edition of the Bible containing both the Old and New Testaments. Avoid translations that use archaic language (like the King James version) or paraphrasing (like the Living Bible). The New American Bible and the Catholic edition of the New Revised Standard Version are good choices.

We strongly recommend using a youth-friendly study Bible such as *The Catholic Youth Bible,* published by Saint Mary's Press. Such Bibles commonly contain helpful background articles and introductions to individual books of the Bible that can enrich the participants' knowledge and discussion.

Where and When Should I Use These Sessions?

The most natural place to use the *ScriptureWalk Junior High* sessions is in junior high youth group meetings, which is what they were originally designed for. However, with a little creativity, you can find many other uses for the sessions or for the activities within each session. Consider these uses:

- as part of your religious education program
- as part of a weekly Scripture study group
- as a component of a miniretreat
- as a supplement to the reflections included in *The Catholic Youth Bible*
- as a recipe book from which you can pick and choose individual parts to add pizzazz to your Scripture class
- as a homily help when you are preparing to celebrate liturgy with junior high young people

The order of the session themes in this ScriptureWalk volume loosely correspond to the calendar as well as the liturgical year. Thus, for example, the theme of the first session, "Living in the Light," is an appropriate theme to begin a new program year, and the theme of session 7, "The Spirit's Promise," would be appropriate at the end of the year near the feast of Pentecost. The themes also reflect the changing dynamics of a group as the participants continue to meet each month and grow more comfortable with discussion.

What Group Size Works with These Sessions?

The time estimates for the session activities are based on a group size of ten to fifteen young people. However, by slightly adjusting the session plans, they can be used with groups as small as five or as large as sixty. For example, when doing a discussion exercise with a large group, invite only a limited number of participants to share their thoughts. Or break the large group into smaller groups. Look over the session plan in advance to determine which activities will work better with a large group and which will work better with small groups.

Comprehensive Youth Ministry

The *ScriptureWalk Junior High* sessions are designed to be used as part of a comprehensive or total youth ministry program. This model acknowledges that a well-rounded program for youth includes educational, social, service, and spiritual opportunities. This resource aims to meet these needs as follows.

Educational. This material is catechetical, but uses an informal teaching model. The sessions introduce and reinforce knowledge of the Scriptures, invite young people to spend more time reading the Bible, and explore issues critical to young people today.

Social. These sessions are an opportunity for young people to gather and share their faith in a nonthreatening environment. Designed with variety and a sense of surprise, the activities are meant to be fun. Many of them also build and strengthen community.

Service. The Gospel messages call young people to look beyond themselves to serve God and others. Some sessions invite the young people to serve others during the meeting. Others ask the young people to reflect on or discuss their approach to poor and lost people in today's society.

Spiritual. Prayer is one of the three critical components in each session, yet spirituality is not confined to one activity. It is woven throughout the various activities. The young people are challenged to take the messages they learn from the Scriptures and weave them through their own life.

Session Leaders

The sessions in this manual do not need to be led by professional ministers. They are designed to be used by volunteers with a minimum of training. They contain complete directions that when followed will help ensure a successful session. They do require preparation, though. Whoever is leading them must be sure to read the session over several times and think through the particulars of their situation. To help you plan, each session includes several materials needed lists—one overall list for the whole session and an individual list for each activity. Also included with each session is a checklist of other necessary preparations.

These sessions are also a good place to involve your high school youth leaders. At Holy Spirit Parish, older teens facilitated the small groups and the adult leaders introduced, facilitated, and processed each activity. Appendix B, "Guidelines for Small-Group Leaders," is offered to help your group leaders facilitate small groups.

The Bible Is a Library, Not a Book

The Bible is filled with many different types of writing. God is revealed not only in narrative but also in poetry and drama, in epic stories and letters. We have a tendency sometimes to stick with what we know well. But if we preach only from the Gospels, we miss out on the inspiration of the letters later in the New Testament. If we read only the New Testament, we miss out on the richness and texture of our roots in the Old Testament.

The Bible is not homework for a speed-reading class. The Bible isn't just the study notes for the big Catholic exam in the sky that we'll all have to pass some day, or even a program to store on the desktop of a computer. The Bible is to be sampled and savored and read over again and again.

There is no right or wrong way to read the Bible. Some people read it from cover to cover. Others drop in here and there as the Spirit inspires them to turn the pages. These sessions do not give young people a formula on how to read the Bible. It is an intensely personal decision. My hope is that young people may begin to look at the Bible as a companion for the journey—a place that they can return to again and again—to search for guidance, to celebrate, to find comfort, and to constantly learn.

One of the most amazing things about the Bible is that we can read the same Scripture passage over and over again and yet we continue to be inspired in different ways. Take, for example, the parable of the prodigal son. Sometimes when we read this Scripture, we are the prodigal in need of forgiveness from God and others. Another time we might be the father, the one who reaches out with forgiveness. Yet another time we might be the other brother, the one who just cannot let go of a grudge. And on a particularly rough day, we might feel like the pigs. Even the Scriptures can have a sense of humor.

Understanding that the Bible contains many different styles of writing is part of interpreting the Bible's message in its proper context. Interpreting each passage of the Bible in its total context is central to the way Catholics understand the Bible. For an excellent overview of how Catholics interpret the Bible, read the article in appendix A, "What the Scriptures Say . . . and Don't Say: Reading the Bible in Context."

A Few Words on the Lectionary

For many Catholics—including young people—exposure to the Bible comes primarily at Mass, when the Scriptures are read from the lectionary. Each Sunday in the lectionary includes three readings and a psalm. The first reading is typically from the Old Testament and is selected to relate with the Gospel reading. The psalm usually complements the first reading and the Gospel. The second reading is from one of the letters of the Apostles. The third reading is taken from one of the four Gospels.

At the end of each session, you will find a list of lectionary references so that you can match the themes of the sessions with different Sundays of the year. This will be particularly helpful if your youth group bases each of its meeting themes on the readings of the previous Sunday, or if the religious education department at your parish uses a lectionary-based program.

Making the Scriptures Come Alive for You

If we want young people to spend more time with the Bible, we must do the same—and not just when we look up a passage while preparing for a youth group meeting.

Try to find time before your session to read and reflect on the Scripture passages you will be using. This way, your introductions and process time will be less "textbook" and more from the heart. You can also make a point of reflecting on the lectionary readings before or after weekend liturgy at your parish.

Read the Scriptures.

Proclaim the Scriptures.

Remember that you may be the only Gospel the young people in your group ever hear.

My prayer is that the Scriptures come alive through you,
that the Spirit inspire your ministry,
and that you may see the Gospel in the lives of your young people.

Suggested Resources

An overwhelming number of resources for studying the Bible are available. I have reviewed many of them and recommend the following resources to leaders and groups using *ScriptureWalk Junior High:*

Achtemeier, Paul J., gen. ed. *HarperCollins Bible Dictionary.* [San Francisco]: HarperSanFrancisco, 1996. Provides helpful information on people, places, and concepts in the Bible.

Bergant, Dianne, and Robert J. Karris, gen. eds. *Collegeville Bible Commentary.* Collegeville, MN: Liturgical Press, 1989. Gives detailed information and interpretation for each book in the Bible.

The Bible Library for Catholics. Liguori Software, 800-325-9521. This computer CD-ROM has three complete Catholic translations of the Bible, Nave's Topical Index, search software, and more.

Catucci, Thomas F. *Time with Jesus: Guided Meditations for Youth.* Notre Dame, IN: Ave Maria Press, 1993.

Hamma, Robert M., ed. *A Catechumen's Lectionary.* Mahwah, NJ: Paulist Press, 1988.

Ralph, Margaret Nutting. *"And God Said What?" An Introduction to Biblical Literary Forms for Bible Lovers.* New York: Paulist Press, 1986. A wonderful introduction to interpreting the Bible from a contextualist approach.

Sanchez, Patricia Datchuk. *The Word We Celebrate: Commentary on the Sunday Lectionary. Years A, B, and C.* Kansas City, MO: Sheed and Ward, 1989.

Scripture from Scratch: A Popular Guide to Understanding the Bible. Cincinnati: Saint Anthony Messenger Press. A monthly newsletter.

Session 1

Living in the Light

Objectives

This session has three objectives:

- To help the young people recognize Jesus as the light for all the world
- To invite them to choose to walk in the light
- To challenge them to be light for others

Background on the Session Theme

In this session Jesus, the light for the world, calls us to recognize and celebrate the light that shines in each of us. The reading from Matthew 5:14–16 (used in the activity "We Can Be Light for Others") is a tremendous affirmation for each of us. It is as if Jesus took a giant spotlight and placed it on each person and said, "Look at this great, wonderful person I have created." Yet this light comes with responsibility. We cannot hide or squander it. We need to share it, to spread it to others.

Young people often struggle with self-worth. They can have a difficult time recognizing their gifts and talents. We, as adults, need to help them coax that flicker of faith into a mighty flame—one that shines for Christ.

Another passage used in this session, Psalm 27, tells us, "The LORD is my light and my salvation" (verse 1). We acknowledge Jesus as the light that guides our way. We recognize that it is only through following God that we will be saved, that we will overcome the darkness in our world. Isaiah 9:2 tells us that the people who walked in darkness have seen a great light. We live in a world where darkness often surrounds us, where sometimes the light must struggle to shine.

But we have a choice. We can choose to remain in the dark or to walk in the light of Christ. Youth today can easily get caught up in the culture of death—from violent video games to dark music to gruesome movies. We can help them choose the light of Christ and gain courage to share that light with others.

Schedule at a Glance

Session Activities (Total session time: 90 minutes)

A. **Introduction** (5 minutes)

B. **Light-Hearted Icebreaker** (10 minutes), a small-group icebreaker

C. **Walking in Darkness** (20 minutes), a small-group discussion

D. **The Lord Is the Light that Never Goes Out** (15 minutes), a reflection and snack break

E. **We Can Be Light for Others** (20 minutes), a reflection and small-group discussion

F. **The Lord Is My Light and My Salvation** (20 minutes), a large-group flashlight prayer

Materials Needed

This is a list of materials needed for all the activities in this session, except the optional activity:

- ☐ flashlights, one for each person
- ☐ index cards
- ☐ different-colored markers
- ☐ Bibles, one for each person
- ☐ a pair of scissors
- ☐ large pieces of black construction paper, two for each small group
- ☐ transparent tape
- ☐ chalk, one piece for each small group

- ☐ a sheet cake decorated with a lighthouse and the Scripture passage "The LORD is my light and my salvation" (Psalm 27:1)
- ☐ trick birthday candles (those that reignite after you blow them out)
- ☐ matches
- ☐ a knife
- ☐ forks, plates, and napkins, one of each for each person
- ☐ a cross
- ☐ pens or pencils
- ☐ copies of handout 1–A, "We Are the Light of the World," one for each small group

Other Necessary Preparations

- ☐ *For activity B.* Identify Scripture passages that include the word *light.* You will need one for each small group. Some examples are given in activity B.
- ☐ *For activity C.* Tape together side-by-side two pieces of black construction paper for each small group.
- ☐ Review the optional activity at the end of this session and consider whether you would like to use it in some way, for example, in place of another activity, as a way to extend the session, or as a follow-up activity.

Session Activities

Activity A

Introduction (5 minutes)

Materials needed. flashlights

1. Before the youth enter the meeting room, dim the lights, leaving just enough light to find a seat. Leave flashlights in various places around the room, but give no instructions. Observe what the young people do with the flashlights—whether they ignore them, turn them on, shine them at one another, make patterns with the light on the ceiling, and so on.

2. Introduce the session in these or similar words:

- Are you afraid of the dark? Most of us are old enough to know that no monsters lurk under our bed, yet most of us feel better when some light is on in the room. When you enter a dark room, what is usually the first thing you do? Turn on the light? Why? When you came into our room tonight, what did you do with the flashlights? Did you want to shed some light on the matter?

  Light is a symbol of hope. Nightlights help us feel safer. Lighthouses once guided ships lost at sea. Christmas lights celebrate the birth of Christ. Fireworks excite and surprise, and candles on a birthday cake cause us to sing. We light candles to celebrate our faith and pray to God.

Light has been an important part of people's faith, from the early worshipers who prayed to God in the sun to Catholic Christians today who light candles at Mass on Sunday. In this session we will learn more about Jesus, the light for the world. We will be challenged to choose a path of light rather than to walk in darkness, and we will be called to be light for others.

Activity B — Light-Hearted Icebreaker (10 minutes)

Related Scripture passages. passages that include the word *light,* for example, Isaiah 9:2; Psalm 27:1; Matthew 5:14–16; John 1:5; Ephesians 5:8

Materials needed. index cards; different-colored markers; Bibles, one for each person; a pair of scissors

Before the session. Identify Scripture passages that include the word *light.* You will need one for each small group. Some examples follow:

"You are the light of the world" (Matthew 5:14).

"The LORD is my light and my salvation" (Psalm 27:1).

"Let your light shine before others" (Matthew 5:16).

"Live as children of light" (Ephesians 5:8).

"The light shines in the darkness, and the darkness did not overcome it" (John 1:5).

"The people who walked in darkness / have seen a great light" (Isaiah 9:2).

Estimate how many people you will have in each small group. Assign one passage to each small group and divide it into as many segments as there are members of the small group. Include the citation with the last phrase. For example, if five people are in a group, you might divide the following phrase as marked: "The Light shines / in the darkness, / and the darkness / did not overcome / it" (John 1:5). Write each segment of a passage on a separate index card, using the same color of marker for each segment. Repeat the process for each Scripture passage that you chose, but use a different-colored pen for each passage. After you have created cards for all the Scripture passages, scramble all the cards.

1. Introduce the session with comments like the following:

- Our meeting tonight is about light, how Jesus is the light of the world. As we begin our meeting, I would like you to think a little about the theme of light and how important it is in our life.

Divide the young people into small groups based on your estimate of how many people would be in each. Distribute at random the cards that you prepared before the session. Be prepared to cut a card or two in half if you don't have enough. Of, if you have too many cards, give one or more people two cards.

2. Ask the young people to find people whose cards have words that are the same color as the card they hold. When they think they have everyone together, they should unscramble the phrase and stand in order with their cards.

3. Ask each group to find their passage in the Bible and read before and after the verse to discover its context. Ask them to spend 5 minutes discussing the meaning that the Scripture passage might hold for them.

4. Ask a spokesperson from each small group to share what her or his group discovered.

Activity C Walking in Darkness (20 minutes)

Related Scripture passage. Isaiah 9:2

Materials needed. Bibles, one for each person; large pieces of black construction paper, two for each small group; transparent tape; chalk, one piece for each small group

Before the session. Tape together side-by-side two pieces of black construction paper for each small group.

1. Read aloud Isaiah 9:2 and introduce this activity with comments along the following lines:

- In this Scripture passage, we hear about people who lived in darkness. In today's world we also live surrounded by darkness. We often call these influences sin or the temptation to sin. This is how evil finds its way into the world. We need to become more aware of the darkness all around us so that we are better able to stay away from the darkness and rather walk in the light.

2. Give each small group a piece of chalk and the black construction paper that you prepared before the session. Assign each group a different aspect of modern culture that they are most likely to be familiar with. Some possibilities include music, magazines, newspapers, video games, movies, and television.

3. Direct each group to brainstorm examples of darkness from its assigned category. For example, one group might name a movie that glorifies violence, or another might name a song with racist lyrics. Let each group select a recorder to write with the chalk its examples of sin on the black paper. Make sure each group has at least ten examples before moving on.

4. Gather everyone together and talk about the different examples of darkness from the lists. Solicit specific examples of how these sins can be avoided. Close by reminding the young people that they have a choice, and they can choose to walk in the light rather than walk amid the darkness in our world.

Activity D — The Lord Is the Light that Never Goes Out (15 minutes)

Related Scripture passage. Psalm 27:1

Materials needed. a sheet cake decorated with a lighthouse and the Scripture passage, "The LORD is my light and my salvation" (Psalm 27:1); trick birthday candles (those that reignite after you blow them out); matches; a knife; forks, plates, and napkins, one of each for each person

1. Place trick birthday candles on a sheet cake that you have had decorated with a lighthouse and the Scripture passage, "The LORD is my light and my salvation" (Psalm 27:1). Light the candles.

2. Ask for a volunteer from the group to come forward and try to blow out the candles. When this person fails to keep the candles blown out, ask a second person to come forward and try to blow out the candles.

When this person also fails, ask the participants how they can compare the candles to the way Jesus lights up our life every day. Make the point that even when we struggle with darkness, Jesus is the light who will never go out.

3. Then take a snack break and enjoy the cake.

Activity E — We Can Be Light for Others (20 minutes)

Related Scripture passage. Matthew 5:14–16

Materials needed. Bibles, one for each person; a cross; pens or pencils; copies of handout 1–A, "We Are the Light of the World," one for each small group; different-colored markers

1. Direct everyone to regather into their small group. Give each teen a pen or pencil and provide each small group with a copy of handout 1–A, "We Are the Light of the World."

2. Proclaim Matthew 5:14–16. Then introduce this activity with comments along the following lines:

- This passage tells us that the light of Christ shines so bright that it shines through each of us. Jesus says we, too, are the light of the world. It is our call to spread the light of Christ through our words and actions.

3. Direct the young people to each think of one way—through words or actions—that they can be the light of Christ for others. You may want to give them a few examples. Then tell them to choose a candle on their group's copy of the handout, color it in with a marker, and write around or near their candle's flame their idea for how to share the light. Suggest that they also sign their name to the handout.

4. After the young people are finished, tell them that you will hang their "We Are the Light of the World" posters where members of the parish can see them.

Activity F

The Lord Is My Light and My Salvation (20 minutes)

Related Scripture passage. Psalm 27:1

Materials needed. a Bible; flashlights, ideally one for each person (collect as many as you can, or ask the young people to bring one of their own), including a large one for the leader

1. As you usher the young people into the area you plan to use for prayer, hand each of them a flashlight, directing them to keep it *off.* Have them sit in a circle. Darken the lights in the prayer space, and turn on one large flashlight.

2. Begin by reading Psalm 27:1. Ask the young people to think of one prayer that they would like to offer tonight, asking God to send light to someone in need—someone in their family, at school, or anyone throughout the world. Go around the circle and ask each teen, one at a time, to offer a brief petition or prayer. After a person offers a petition or prayer, he or she may turn on his or her flashlight.

3. After all have had a chance to pray, reflect on how dark the room was before the prayer and how bright it is after they called on God. Encourage the young people to continue turning to God and asking God to shine on their life.

Optional Activity

Light Catchers (30 minutes)

Related Scripture passage. 1 John 1:5

Materials needed. red, yellow, and orange tissue paper; several pairs of scissors; waxed paper; Mod-podge shellac; medium-size paint brushes; 5-by-5-inch slips of paper, one for each person; pens; red pipe cleaners, one for each person; glue; a hole puncher; red yarn

Before the session. Cut sheets of red, yellow, and orange tissue paper into 1-by-1-inch pieces. Cut enough 12-by-12-inch sheets of waxed paper so that each teen has one sheet. Make a sample light catcher to show the young people before they begin the project (see the step-by-step directions below).

1. Introduce this activity with comments like the following:

- During the next part of our meeting, you will have a chance to let your light shine to cheer up our parish shut-ins by making light catchers for them. Please do a really nice job with them because they will mean a lot to people, especially those who rarely get visitors or gifts. This is a way you can be the light of Christ to people you have never met.

2. Show the participants the sample light catcher that you created before the session. Distribute a sheet of waxed paper to each person, set out the other supplies, and give the young people the following step-by-step directions on how to make a light catcher:

- Cover the center of your sheet of waxed paper with squares of tissue paper, making sure the squares overlap only a little bit, creating a stained-glass effect.
- Use a paint brush to cover the work with a thin layer of Mod-podge shellac. Allow it to dry.
- On a 5-by-5-inch slip of paper, write "God is light and in him there is no darkness (1 John 1:5)." Punch a hole in the end of the slip.
- Shape a pipe cleaner into a heart and glue it on top of the stained-glass creation.
- Trim the excess waxed paper and tissue paper around the outside edge of the heart.
- Punch a hole in the top of the heart and put a piece of red yarn through the slip of paper and the heart, to use as a hanger.

Scripture References

Additional Scripture Passages

Genesis 1:1–4. Let there be light.
John 3:19–21. Come into the light.
John 8:12. "I am the light of the world."
John 12:35–36. Walk in the light.
1 John 1:5. God is light.

Lectionary Readings

Cycle A
Third Sunday of Ordinary Time
Fifth Sunday of Ordinary Time
Fourth Sunday of Lent

Cycle B
Fourth Sunday of Lent
Third Sunday of Advent

Cycle C
Second Sunday After Christmas

Session Follow-Up

Family Connection

Suggest to the young people that they try the following activity at home. Make copies of the directions to send home with them.

> Send family members (of all ages) on a scavenger hunt through their home to find items that represent light or shed light. Some examples: a flashlight, a candle, a nightlight, a lamp, a penlight, Christmas lights, a sparkler, matches, a skylight, a sun catcher, a sunflower.
>
> Gather the items together (if possible) on a table with family members sitting around the table. Ask each person to choose an item and make up a prayer to go with it. This is often called common-object meditation.
>
> Two prayer examples follow:
>
> > Lord, help me be like this sun catcher, willing to catch the light of Christ and allow Jesus to shine through me to others.
> >
> > • • •
> >
> > Lord, help me be like this sparkler, full of surprise and excitement and willing to light up the world for others.
>
> When everyone is finished, read together Matthew 5:14–16. Close with a family affirmation, identifying ways your family is light for others.

We Are the Light of the World

Handout 1–A: Permission to reproduce this handout for session use is granted.

Session 2

Making Change

Objectives

This session has three objectives:

- To encourage the young people to make new friends and feel more comfortable with the people in their youth group
- To challenge them to reflect on the way they spend money
- To invite them to think about their relationship with God and to consider whether they need to make a change to put God first

Background on the Session Theme

The main Scripture passage used in this session is Matthew 22:15–21. In it the Pharisees try to trap Jesus and end up being an object lesson about the priorities in our life and where God fits in.

The Pharisees knew that taxes were unpopular, so they figured Jesus would get in trouble either way he answered their question, "Is it lawful to pay taxes to the emperor, or not?" (verse 17). If Jesus said not to pay taxes, he'd be in trouble with Rome. If he said to pay taxes, he would be unpopular with the Jews. In reply Jesus embarrassed the questioners by showing that they carried coins with the emperor's image—which was considered idolatry by strict Jews. He then gave the deceptively simple answer, "Give therefore to the emperor the things that are the emperor's, and to God the things that are God's" (verse 21). Giving to God what is God's can be very difficult sometimes to figure out. But it starts with the commitment to do so.

The other Scriptures used in this session challenge us to put God first in our life and to remember to praise, honor, and worship God. Isaiah 45:4–6 echoes one of the Ten Commandments. It also tells us that God calls us by name. God gives us all we have, so all we become is our thanksgiving to God. In 1 Thessalonians 1:1–3, Paul is thankful for the new church in Thessalonica. The Christians in Thessalonica put God first; they put the Gospel first. One way we can praise God is by thanking God for the gift of others in our life. Paul is thankful for the faith, hope, and love found in the new church in Thessalonica.

Our culture of materialism often targets teens and preteens, many of whom have a good deal of discretionary income. We need to pose some tough questions to young people: Have you left any time for God in your busy schedule? Do you give more honor and glory to a favorite football team? Do you give more glory to a love for shopping? How can you do a better job of giving to God what is God's?

Schedule at a Glance

Session Activities (Total session time: 90 minutes)

A. **Introduction** (5 minutes)

B. **Shoe Name Game** (15 minutes), a large-group icebreaker

C. **Spending Money** (20 minutes), a small-group activity and large-group discussion

D. **Snack Break** (10 minutes)

E. **Neglecting Our Relationship with God?** (20 minutes), a large-group activity

F. **Praying with Change** (20 minutes), a large-group prayer and song

Materials Needed

This is a list of materials needed for all the activities in this session, except the optional activity:

- ☐ a coin
- ☐ blank name tags
- ☐ markers
- ☐ Bibles, one for each person
- ☐ catalogs, one large one or several smaller ones for each small group

- ☐ white paper
- ☐ pens or pencils
- ☐ play money, two hundred dollars (in bills of twenty dollars or less) for each small group
- ☐ snacks
- ☐ two pieces of poster board
- ☐ a pair of scissors
- ☐ masking tape
- ☐ coins (pennies, nickels, dimes, and quarters), one for each person
- ☐ song sheets for a song of your choice
- ☐ small, inexpensive piggy banks (or the rice bowls used by many parishes during Lent), one for each person

Other Necessary Preparations

- ☐ *For activity E.* Cut out a large circle from each of two pieces of poster board. Put a likeness of Caesar on one and a cross on the other, leaving enough room to write on the coins later. Tape them to a wall in your meeting room.
- ☐ *For activity F.* Choose a song that relates to today's readings and the theme of making change in our life. Designate a song leader to help you lead the prayer.
- ☐ Review the optional activity at the end of this session and consider whether you would like to use it in some way, for example, in place of another activity, as a way to extend the session, or as a follow-up activity.

Session Activities

Activity A

Introduction (5 minutes)

Related Scripture passage. Matthew 22:15–21

Materials needed. a coin

Flip a coin—a quarter probably works best—and ask the young people to call it, heads or tails. You may have to flip it a few times, but when it comes up heads, begin your meeting by saying the following:

- Whose head is on a quarter? In Jesus' day the Roman emperor Caesar was on many of the coins. The Gospel story in our session starts with a debate about what God should get and what Caesar should get. We also have a lot of things competing with God for our time and attention in today's world. We'll talk about what we give to God and what we devote all the rest of our time and energy to. Is it possible that God sometimes ends up with nothing but our small change?

If the young people have change with them, invite them to hold on to it to reflect on throughout the meeting, especially during the closing prayer. Tell them that during this session they will have the chance to reflect on change and to pray for change.

Activity B Shoe Name Game (15 minutes)

This is a good game to play at the start of the year, when the group is new. If your young people all know one another, substitute the optional activity "Psalm Scramble," found at the end of this session plan.

Related Scripture passage. Isaiah 45:4–6

Materials needed. blank name tags, markers, a Bible

1. Have everyone fill out and put on a name tag. Then ask them to stand in a circle, shoulder to shoulder. Instruct them to take off one shoe and place it on the floor right in front of them.

2. Ask a teen to read aloud Isaiah 45:4–6 to the group. Then comment along the following lines:

- In this reading from the prophet Isaiah, God is telling a foreign king, Cyrus, that God has called him by name even though he does not know who God is. God knew us by name and called us by name, too, before we were even aware of God. Some of you attended these sessions last year, others are new to the parish [or school]. Still others just entered sixth grade and are now part of our group. Each of you is wearing a name tag already. Another way we can learn who everyone is, so that we can call each other by name, is to play a name game. This one is called the "Shoe Name Game."

3. Remove one shoe from the circle. Ask the shoe's owner to stand in the middle of the circle. Tell the young people that when they are in the middle of the circle, they must (a) say their name, (b) tell one thing about themselves (for example, I am in seventh grade or I have two brothers or I like pizza), and (c) call out one characteristic several people might have in common and direct those people to switch places (for example, "Everyone wearing glasses, switch").

Explain that after the person in the middle calls out the characteristic, he or she and everyone to whom that characteristic applies must leave their spot and go stand by a vacant shoe. The person who doesn't have a spot must stand in the middle of the circle and begin the process again as noted above.

4. After playing for 10 to 12 minutes, invite anyone who has not been in the middle to introduce herself or himself to the group. Encourage the young people to continue getting to know one another during the rest of the meeting and other times they gather together.

Activity C Spending Money (20 minutes)

Related Scripture passage. 1 Thessalonians 1:1–3

Materials needed. catalogs, one large one or several smaller ones for each small group; pens or pencils; white paper; play money, two hundred dollars (in bills of twenty dollars or less) for each small group

1. Give each small group one large catalog or several smaller catalogs, a pen or pencil, and paper. Direct each group to choose someone to be the recorder (to do the writing for the group) and someone to be the spokesperson (to do the speaking for the group).

2. Give each group two hundred dollars in play money. Tell the participants that they have 10 minutes to go shopping in the catalog. They must decide what to buy as a group. The recorder should write down what the team bought and the cost of each item. The purchases must not go over two hundred dollars.

3. After 10 minutes, gather the young people together into the large group. Ask the spokesperson from each group to report how the money was spent.

4. Discuss the results with the following questions:

- How many of you bought things for yourselves?
- How many of you bought things for others?
- How many of you bought things for needy people?
- How can we use part of our allowance to help other people?

5. Close by reading 1 Thessalonians 1:1–3 to the group. Tell the young people that Paul was thankful to the Thessalonians because they put God first. Stress that God calls us to think not only about ourselves but about others. We give glory and honor to God by serving others.

Activity D Snack Break (10 minutes)

Activity E Neglecting Our Relationship with God? (20 minutes)

Related Scripture passage. Matthew 22:15–21

Materials needed. two pieces of poster board; a pair of scissors; masking tape; markers; Bibles, one for each person

Before the session. Create two giant coins by cutting out a large circle from each of two pieces of poster board. Put a likeness of Caesar on one and a cross on the other, leaving enough room to write on the coins later. Tape them to a wall in your meeting room.

1. Ask the young people to open their Bible and read Matthew 22:15–21. Then ask,

- What do you think Jesus meant when he said, "Give therefore to the emperor the things that are the emperor's, and to God the things that are God's"?

One way of looking at this passage is to explore the things we put before God and the excuses we make for not spending time with God. Ask the young people for examples of such things and excuses and write them with marker on the poster coin bearing Caesar's likeness. Ask them if they can think of a modern person or position that functions as Caesar today.

2. What are some of the ways we can give to God what is God's? Ask the young people for examples and write them with marker on the poster coin bearing the cross.

3. Close by encouraging the young people to make time for God in their everyday life.

Activity F Praying with Change (20 minutes)

Materials needed. coins (pennies, nickels, dimes, and quarters), one for each person; song sheets for a song of your choice; small, inexpensive piggy banks (or the rice bowls used by many parishes during Lent), one for each person

Before the session. Choose a song that relates to today's readings and the theme of making change in our life. Designate a song leader to help you lead the prayer.

1. If the young people are unfamiliar with the song you have selected, you may want to practice it with them before the prayer time.

2. When you call everyone to the prayer area, tell them to bring a coin with them. Have spare change ready in case some people do not have coins. Direct everyone to sit on the floor in small circles of four to five people each. Do not spread them out too far so the participants can see and hear the song leader and the prayer leader. Distribute the song sheets.

3. Explain why you chose the song that you did and how it relates to today's readings. Then invite the designated song leader to help you lead the group in the following prayer:

Song leader. [Lead the young people in one or two verses of the song.]

Prayer leader. In today's Gospel, Jesus uses a small Roman coin as a way to teach. Today we are going to use our coins as a way to pray.

In your small group, I'd like each of you to offer a short prayer. If you have a **penny,** offer a prayer for yourself. If you have a **nickel,** offer a prayer for your friends. If you have a **dime,** offer a prayer for your family. If you have a **quarter,** offer a prayer of thanks to God.

[When all the groups are finished praying, give each teen a small piggy bank (or a rice bowl like those used by many parishes during Lent).]

Prayer leader. Today we talked about how to spend our money for others and not for ourselves. We also talked about giving glory and honor to God. One of the ways we honor God is by serving others. We also used coins as a way to pray.

Take this bank home and put it in your room. Every night when you pray, place a coin in the bank. When it is full, take the money and use it to serve others. For example, give the money to the food pantry or buy a card for someone in the hospital.

Song leader. [Sing two more verses of the song used above.]

Optional Activity

Psalm Scramble (20 minutes)

Related Scripture passage. Psalm 96

Materials needed. newspapers, a pile for each small group; scissors, two pair for each small group; glue, one bottle for each small group; continuous-feed computer paper, a long sheet for each small group; 8½-by-11-inch copy paper, one sheet for each small group

Before the session. Write the phrase "Give the Lord glory and honor," from Psalm 96, on a piece of 8½-by-11-inch paper. Make a copy for each small group.

1. Divide the participants into groups of six to eight people. Give each group a pile of newspapers, two pairs of scissors, a bottle of glue, a long sheet of continuous-feed computer paper, and a copy of the Psalm 96 phrase that you prepared.

2. Challenge the young people to work together as a group to spell out the psalm with words or letters from headlines. Allow all the groups to finish, but acknowledge the group that finishes first.

Affirm the young people for working well together in groups. Tell them how small-group sharing is part of every session and encourage them all to participate and support one another.

Scripture References

Additional Scripture Passages

Psalm 95. Praise God with joy and thanksgiving.
Isaiah 49:14–15. God will never forget us.
Matthew 6:24–34. Which master do you serve? Put God first.
Matthew 7:21–27. Put faith into action.
Matthew 10:26–33. God has counted every one of your hairs.
Luke 12:13–21. The rich fool
Luke 16:1–13. We can't serve God and money.
Acts of the Apostles 3:13–15,17–19. Change your ways.
1 John 3:18–24. Faith must take action.

Lectionary Readings

Cycle A
Eighth Sunday of Ordinary Time
Twenty-ninth Sunday of Ordinary Time

Cycle C
Eighteenth Sunday of Ordinary Time
Twenty-fifth Sunday of Ordinary Time
Twenty-sixth Sunday of Ordinary Time

Session Follow-Up

Family Connection

Suggest to the young people that they try the following activity at home. Make copies of the directions to send home with them.

Share the following Scripture readings as a family:
Isaiah 45:4–6
1 Thessalonians 1:1–3
Matthew 22:15–21
Psalm 96

Let these Scriptures lead you to take a close look at how you spend money as a family. Some questions to discuss:

- How do we spend money as a family?
- How do we give to God what is God's?
- Do we give as generously as we can to people in need? Do we spend our money without much thought for helping others?

Consider picking a service project to do with your family. Think of ways to help by using the model of time, talent, and treasure:

- *Time.* How can we give of our time—as a family—to help others?
- *Talent.* What gifts do we each have that we can offer to help others?
- *Treasure.* What sacrifices can we make—from our paychecks and allowances—to help others?

Journey

Objectives

This session has three objectives:

- To reinforce in the young people that the Ten Commandments are guides along their journey through life
- To help them learn how to navigate the obstacles in their everyday life that keep them from living as good Christians
- To help them form practical goals of how they can follow the Ten Commandments more closely in their everyday life

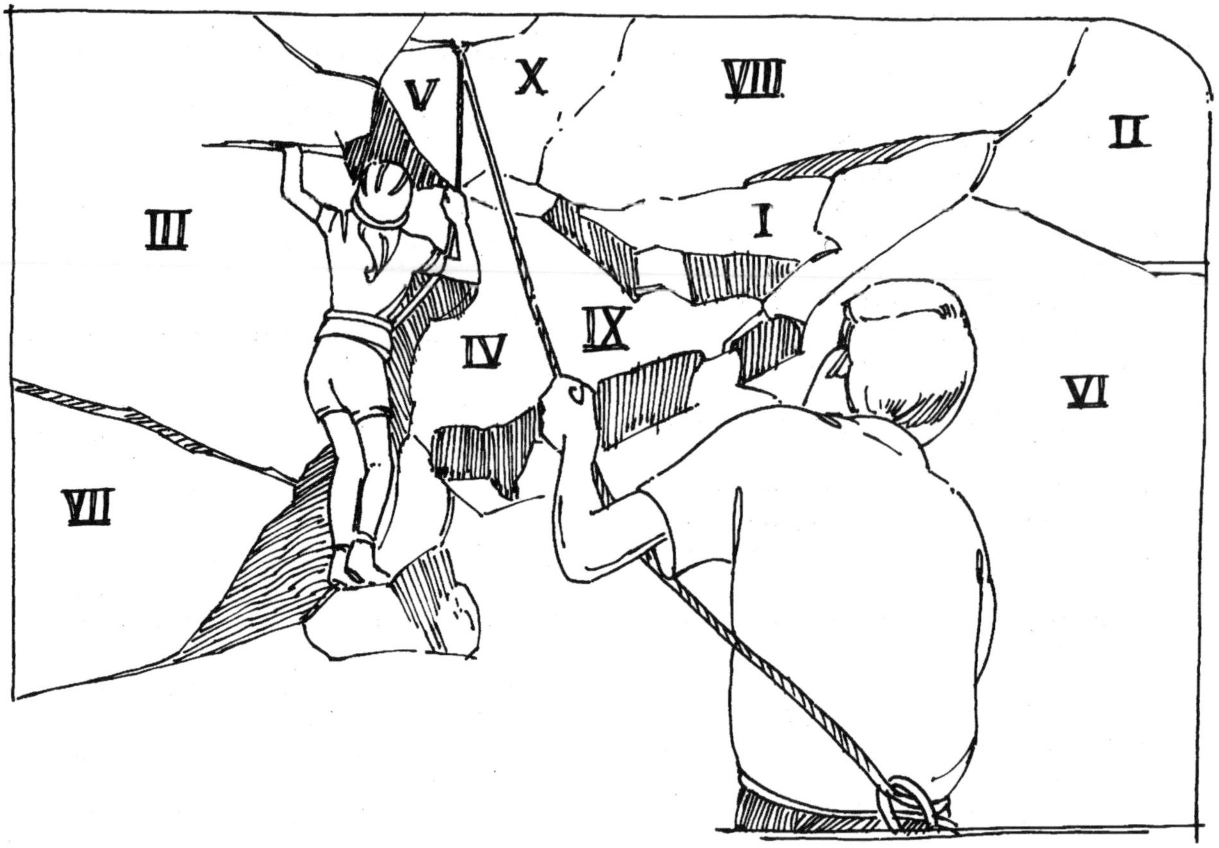

Background on the Session Theme

This session focuses on the Ten Commandments as part of the moral road map God gives us to live happy and holy lives. The activity "Rules, Rules, Rules" uses Exodus 20:1–17 to introduce one of the lists of the Ten Commandments found in the Bible. The activity "Signs Along the Road" moves on to Matthew 5:17–37 where Jesus makes clear his support of the Commandments: "I have come not to abolish [the Law] but to fulfill" (verse 17).

We cannot approach the Ten Commandments like a buffet line—we cannot just pick some laws to follow and ignore the others. Not only are we to live the Commandments, we should be an example for others and teach them. "Whoever does [these Commandments] and teaches them will be called great in the kingdom of heaven" (verse 19).

Psalm 119 is referred to in the activity "Obstacles Along the Road." It tells us that following God's Law is a recipe for happiness. "Happy are those . . . / who follow the law of the Lord" (verse 1). The psalmist asks for help to learn, understand, and keep God's Law "with my whole heart" (verse 10).

Young adolescents may just be starting to chaff at the rules they must follow at home and at school. We can help them understand that rules are needed for living together peacefully and that God's Law is actually the best guide for our life. The Ten Commandments must be more than just a list to memorize. They are our map for living happy, healthy, and holy lives.

The Ten Commandments

The following traditional formula for the Ten Commandments is quoted from the *Catechism of the Catholic Church* and is based on Exodus 20:1–17. I suggest that you use this *Catechism* version of the Commandments throughout the session, but also explain to the young people that it is based on the Exodus passage.

1. I am the LORD your God: you shall not have strange Gods before me.
2. You shall not take the name of the LORD your God in vain.
3. Remember to keep holy the LORD's Day.
4. Honor your father and your mother.
5. You shall not kill.
6. You shall not commit adultery.
7. You shall not steal.
8. You shall not bear false witness against your neighbor.
9. You shall not covet your neighbor's wife.
10. You shall not covet your neighbor's goods.

(*Catechism of the Catholic Church,* pp. 496–497)

Schedule at a Glance

Session Activities (Total session time: 90 minutes)

A. Introduction (5 minutes)

B. Rules, Rules, Rules (20 minutes), a large-group icebreaker on the Ten Commandments

C. Signs Along the Road (15 minutes), a small-group activity

D. **Stretch Break** (10 minutes)

E. **Obstacles Along the Road** (20 minutes), an obstacle course

F. **Following the Cross** (10 minutes), a quiet, individual reflection exercise

G. **Backpack Prayer** (10 minutes), a large-group prayer

Materials Needed

This is a list of materials needed for all the activities in this session, except the optional activity:

- ☐ a variety of maps (brought by the participants)
- ☐ the video *The Ten Commandments,* starring Charlton Heston
- ☐ a television
- ☐ a VCR
- ☐ Bibles, one for each person
- ☐ poster board, one piece for activity B, and a quarter sheet for each small group for activity C
- ☐ a pair of scissors
- ☐ markers, several for each small group
- ☐ masking tape
- ☐ blindfolds, one for each pair of students
- ☐ a roll of butcher paper or some other type of white paper with which to cover a portion of one of your meeting room walls
- ☐ a black marker
- ☐ the road signs created during activity C
- ☐ objects and obstacles for use in creating an obstacle course
- ☐ a road map
- ☐ colored photocopy paper
- ☐ a backpack
- ☐ string
- ☐ index cards
- ☐ a hole puncher
- ☐ *items to put into the backpack:* a small portable cassette or CD player; a watch; a piece of jewelry; a map; a pocket mirror; a small teddy bear; a one-dollar bill; a ball of string; a pair of scissors; a pocket computer or calculator
- ☐ a small table
- ☐ copies of the closing prayer from activity G, one for each person

Other Necessary Preparations

- ☐ *For activity A.* Ask the young people to bring a map to this session.
- ☐ *For activity A.* Cue the video *The Ten Commandments* at the place where God gives Moses the Ten Commandments.
- ☐ *For activity B.* Prepare the commandment strips as directed in activity B.
- ☐ *For activity E.* Cover one wall of your meeting space with white paper and draw a long highway along it with black marker.
- ☐ *For activity E.* Set up an obstacle course as directed in activity E.
- ☐ *For activity F.* Prepare "map crosses" as directed in activity F.
- ☐ *For activity G.* Prepare cards for the backpack items as directed in activity G.

☐ Review the optional activity at the end of this session and consider whether you would like to use it in some way, for example, in place of another activity, as a way to extend the session, or as a follow-up activity.

Session Activities

Activity A

Introduction (5 minutes)

Materials needed. a variety of maps (brought by the participants); the video *The Ten Commandments,* starring Charlton Heston; a television; a VCR

Before the session. Ask the young people to each bring a map of some sort to the session, for example, a guide to seating at a baseball stadium, a map of attractions at a theme park, an ordinary road map, or a map of the state they live in. Rent the video *The Ten Commandments,* starring Charlton Heston. Cue it at the place where God gives Moses the Ten Commandments.

1. Show the video clip where God gives Moses the Ten Commandments. Then ask the young people to show one another the different kinds of maps they brought in and what they are used for. When they are finished ask,
- What map can we use to help us get to heaven?

Hopefully, they will list a few ideas: the Bible, the Beatitudes, the Golden Rule, the Ten Commandments, and so on.

2. Say:
- We'll learn more about the Ten Commandments today, not just how Hollywood portrays them but also how they connect with our everyday lives today, in the twenty-first century.

Activity B

Rules, Rules, Rules (20 minutes)

Related Scripture passage. Exodus 20:1–17

Materials needed. Bibles, one for each person; poster board, one sheet; a pair of scissors; markers; masking tape

Before the session.
- Cut out ten strips of poster board and write on each one a different commandment (see page 33).
- Place a little loop of masking tape on either end of each commandment and tape the pieces of poster board to the wall, with the words facing the wall.
- Place a little loop of masking tape on either end of the blank side of the poster board pieces so that later you will be able to turn them over easily and stick them to the wall with the words showing.

1. Introduce this activity with comments like the following:

- In the Scripture passages for tonight, we will hear about how important it is to follow God's laws. We will also talk about ways we can live God's laws in our everyday life.

  Everyone here has to live by some rules. We have to deal with rules everywhere we go—at home, at school, at church, and so on. Let's start our meeting with an icebreaker called "Rules, Rules, Rules." You may recognize it as a game you played long ago called "Red Light, Green Light."

2. Ask for a volunteer to be the ruler of the game. Direct the ruler to stand near the wall covered with the commandment strips. Direct all the others to stand by the opposite wall.

3. Explain that the ruler may say only one of two phrases, "Go for it" or "Stop or else." When the ruler turns her or his back and says, "Go for it," the young people are allowed to sneak forward and try to tag the ruler. When the ruler says, "Stop or else," and turns around, everyone must freeze in place. If the ruler sees someone moving even just a little, they are sent back to the starting line.

4. When the ruler is tagged, the tagger must name one of the Ten Commandments. If he or she does so correctly, that commandment is turned over on the wall so all can see it. The tagger may then either choose someone else to be the ruler or choose to rule. If the tagger does not name a commandment correctly, he or she goes back to the starting line.

5. Repeat this process until all the Commandments have been uncovered.

6. Gather everyone together by the wall with the Ten Commandments and pose the following questions:

- Who are some of the people who set rules for us?
- Why is it hard sometimes to follow rules set by others?
- Why do we need rules?
- What would happen if everyone lived by the rule "Go for it" and did whatever they wanted?
- One of the rules of this game was "Stop or else." What are some of the consequences we face when we break the rules?

7. Ask the young people to open their Bible and read Exodus 20:1–17 together. Then ask:

- Why do you think God gave the Ten Commandments to the Israelites?
- Why do you think God asks us to follow the Commandments today?

Activity C Signs Along the Road (15 minutes)

Related Scripture passage. Matthew 5:17–37

Materials needed. markers, several for each small group; poster board, a quarter sheet for each small group

1. Introduce this activity with comments like the following:

- One way to look at God's Commandments is to compare them to signs along the road. When you are riding in a car or traveling on your bike, road signs tell us which direction to take, how fast to go, and how to get along with the other cars on the road.

  The Commandments are a lot like road signs for our life. They guide us on how we respond to God and how we get along with other people. During this activity your group will get one of the Commandments and talk about ways you can follow that commandment in your everyday life.

2. Divide the participants into groups of three or four people each. Give each group a quarter sheet of poster board and some markers. Assign one of the Ten Commandments (see page 33) to each group. Use the commandments that you think will most engage your group.

3. Direct the young people to do the following tasks in their small groups:

- Cut poster board in the shape of a street sign, for example, a stop sign, a one-way sign, a yield sign.
- On the top of the sign, write your assigned commandment in everyday language.
- On the rest of the sign, write at least five ways you can better follow this commandment in your everyday life. [Be prepared to give the young people some examples if they get stuck on some of the tougher commandments.]

4. Close this activity by asking everyone to turn to Matthew 5:17–37 in their Bible. Have one of them read the passage aloud as the others follow. Conclude by acknowledging that the Ten Commandments are more than just a list to memorize. We need to learn more about them so that we can live them in our daily life.

Activity D Stretch Break (10 minutes)

Activity E Obstacles Along the Road (20 minutes)

Related Scripture passage. Psalm 119

Materials needed. a roll of butcher paper or some other type of white paper with which to cover a portion of one of your meeting room walls; a black marker; the road signs created during activity C; masking tape; blindfolds, one for each pair of students; objects and obstacles for an obstacle course

Before the session

- Hang a long piece of butcher paper or newsprint horizontally along one wall of your meeting space and use a black marker to draw a long highway on it.
- Set up an obstacle course that includes, for example, a table to crawl under, cones to go around, chairs to climb across, hoops to crawl through, plastic horses to hop over.

1. Read Psalm 119:1–3 to the group. Mention that Psalm 119 is the longest psalm in the Bible and its message is that the secret to a happy life is following God's law. Tell them that they are going to have some fun tonight learning about God's law as taught in the Ten Commandments by navigating an obstacle course. When you are ready to begin, direct the young people to put a few small loops of masking tape on the back of the road signs they created. Invite a pair from one of the small groups to come forward to run the obstacle course. Blindfold one of the partners and tell the other that she or he may not speak while helping the blindfolded person navigate the obstacle course. At the end of the obstacle course, the pair should place its team sign along the road on the wall.

2. When all the pairs are finished and all the signs are on the road, gather the young people together in a large group and pose the following questions:

- How do obstacles sometimes make it hard for us to follow God's way?
- What are some obstacles that keep us from following God?
- How do God's signs and commandments help us navigate life's obstacles?
- How can others help us overcome obstacles in life?

Activity F — Following the Cross (10 minutes)

This activity helps each teen explore the question Which commandment do I need to follow more closely?

Materials needed. a road map, colored photocopy paper, masking tape

Before the session. Place a road map on a photocopier and make copies using colored paper. You will need one for every two people. Cut out two crosses from each of your photocopied maps, using as much of the page as you can. Make a cross for each participant.

1. Introduce this activity by putting the following comments into your own words:

- Tonight we have talked about God's laws, why we need them, and why sometimes it can be tough to follow them. Take a few moments right now to think about the Ten Commandments and choose one that you would like to work harder to follow in the future.

2. While the young people are reflecting quietly, give each one a map-cross with a loop of masking tape on the back.

3. Direct the young people to go up to the paper road on the wall and place their cross near the commandment sign that they want to work more on following, and then return to their seat.

4. Remind the young people that God's laws aren't easy and that we all need to keep working to follow them as best we can with God's help and the help of other people.

Activity G Backpack Prayer (10 minutes)

Related Scripture passage. Mark 10:17–27

Materials needed. a backpack; string; index cards; a hole puncher; a small portable cassette or CD player; a watch; a piece of jewelry; a map; a pocket mirror; a small teddy bear; a one-dollar bill; a ball of string; a pair of scissors; a pocket computer or calculator; a Bible; a small table; copies of the closing prayer from step 3 on the next page, one for each person

Before the session. Write each of the following prayers on a separate index card and use string to attach the card to its corresponding backpack item:

- *a portable cassette or CD player.* Lord, help us to tune out the many distractions in our life and find quiet to listen to you.
- *a watch.* Lord, please help us to slow down the hectic pace we set and teach us how to make time for you.
- *a piece of jewelry.* Lord, please keep us from wanting more and more possessions and putting things before people.
- *a map.* Lord, help us to accept your life plan for us instead of always telling you where we want to go and be.
- *a pocket mirror.* Lord, please help us look inside each person for you instead of always being concerned about outward appearances.
- *a small teddy bear.* Lord, please give us the courage to set aside our insecurities and be willing to take risks in order to follow you.
- *a one-dollar bill.* Lord, please help us to realize that the things of real value in life are not measured by how much they cost.
- *a ball of string.* Lord, help us to set aside any grudges or petty jealousies that tangle up our hearts, and show us that you are the tie that binds.
- *a pair of scissors.* Lord, help us to cut out our bad habits and dependencies and learn how to depend only on you.
- *a pocket computer or calculator.* Lord, help us not to put facts and figures before faith, and teach us to believe even when we cannot see.

Then place the items in the backpack and put the pack on a small table in the center of your prayer space.

1. Gather the participants in a circle around the backpack and introduce the activity with the following comments:

- Tonight, we have talked about the Ten Commandments and Jesus' call to live them in our everyday life. We've seen how they give us guidance in living in a way pleasing to God, and how they help us avoid life's obstacles.

2. Ask one of the young people to read Mark 10:17–27, the parable of the rich young man. Then say,

- Let us join in prayer, asking God to guide us as we follow along our journey and to give us courage to unpack the things that keep us from truly following God.

Ask for volunteers to come forward one at a time to take an item from the backpack, hold it up so all can see what it is, and then read aloud the prayer attached to it. Then have him or her set the item on a table for all to see.

3. Closing prayer:

- Lord, help us to follow your Commandments on our journey through life. Shield us from doubt so that we never put anything or anyone before you. Help us to unpack all the things that put distance between you and ourselves.

  Guide us on our journey so that we may avoid all obstacles as we follow in your footsteps on the way to your Father. Amen! (Adapted from Maryann Hakowski, *Pathways to Praying with Teens,* pages 15–16)

Optional Activity

God's Game Plan (45 minutes)

Related Scripture passage. Exodus 20:1–17

Materials needed. the videotape *God's Game Plan* (Liguori Publications); a television; a VCR; a flip chart; markers, several for each small group; poster board, one piece for each small group; rulers, one for each small group

1. Introduce this activity with the following comments:

- Some people think the Ten Commandments were written by a whole bunch of guys a long time ago and don't really fit in today's modern society. That is far from the truth. The Ten Commandments are not all God's rules, but they are a great place to start, and every one of them has a lot of real-life connections and applications in our life today.

  We're going to watch only part of a video today. The coach in this video does a great job of telling us what the Ten Commandments really mean. We are only going to watch part of the video because you will be asked to finish the video in your own way by creating a poster.

Stop the video after the third commandment.

2. Ask the young people to name the Ten Commandments (see page 33) in order. Write them on a flip chart so that they can be easily seen by all.

3. Form the participants into small groups and give poster board, markers, and a ruler to each small group. Tell the young people that you would like them to finish the video themselves by making a poster to help us understand better what the Commandments mean to us in our everyday life.

4. Ask each group to choose a different commandment and do the following:

- Write the commandment on the top of the poster.
- Answer the question How do we hurt others by breaking this commandment?
- Answer the question What can I do to better follow this commandment?
- Write a prayer asking Jesus' help to follow this commandment.

Encourage the young people to take a broader view of some of the more difficult commandments in order to generate discussion ideas. For example, the group that chose "You shall not kill" could focus on the ways we can support respect for life. Or the group that chose "You shall not commit adultery" could focus on ways to show respect for the sexuality of others and avoid sex outside of marriage.

5. After everyone is finished, invite a spokesperson from each group to share his or her team's poster with the large group.

(This activity is adapted from Maryann Hakowski, *Growing with Jesus,* pages 121–123.)

Scripture References

Additional Scripture Passages

Genesis 12:1–4. Abraham's journey of faith
Romans 12:1–2. Choose God, not just what is popular.
Matthew 22:34–40. Follow the laws of love.
Deuteronomy 5:12–15. Keep holy the Sabbath.
Deuteronomy 4:1–2,6–8. Do more than just hear the law; live it.

Lectionary Readings

Cycle A
Sixth Sunday of Ordinary Time

Cycle B
Third Sunday of Lent
Ninth Sunday of Ordinary Time
Twenty-second Sunday of Ordinary Time
Twenty-eighth Sunday of Ordinary Time

Session Follow-Up

Family Connection

Tell the young people that our parents give us rules for the same reason God gives us rules—God loves us very much; our parents love us very much. During your session invite them to imagine switching roles with their parents and ask them,

- If you had to set forth rules for your children to follow, what would they be?

Try to get a list of at least ten. Then discuss the following with them:

- How are these rules like the ones you must follow now?
- How are they different?
- How many of the rules deal with our relationship with other people?
- How many of the rules deal with our relationship with God?

Suggest to the young people that they try the following activity at home. Make copies of the directions to send home with them.

> See how many of the Ten Commandments your family can name. If you are having trouble, look them up together in Exodus 20:1–17. After naming or looking up the Ten Commandments, discuss together the following questions:
>
> - How do our family rules relate to God?
> - Even if they don't specifically refer to God, are they expressions of God's law in the Ten Commandments?

Session 4

Being Thankful

Objectives

This session has three objectives:

- To help the young people foster an appreciation of God's many blessings
- To recognize with them that like the ten lepers we all feel rejected sometimes (although God never rejects us)
- To give them an opportunity to offer thanks to God

Background on the Session Theme

The Scriptures in this session call us to recognize God's loving hand in all we are and in all we will be. In the activity "From A to Z," Psalm 92 is used to remind the young people to give thanks to God in prayer and song for God's kindness, faithfulness, and steadfastness—for being the Rock in our lives. "It is good to give thanks to the LORD" (Psalm 92:1).

The story of Jesus' cure of the ten lepers, found in Luke 17:11–16, is the focus for most of the session. Leprosy was a most feared disease in Jesus' day. People were even more afraid of it than we are of AIDS today. People with leprosy not only suffered a painful, crippling, and disfiguring disease but also were made outcasts in society. Families even rejected family members afflicted with leprosy.

So Jesus' cure of the ten lepers was a miracle that completely changed their lives. Yet when they realized that they were cured, only one came back to offer thanks to Jesus. Maybe the other nine were just so excited and overwhelmed by the miracle that they forgot to return. Maybe they just had bad manners. The Scriptures do not tell us why they failed to give thanks to Jesus.

In another passage used in this session, Mark 6:1–6, we see that even the people in Jesus' hometown were unable to recognize and be grateful for the wonderful presence of Jesus in their midst. At Jesus' homecoming there was no red carpet, no homecoming parade, not even a seat in the synagogue. The people's lack of faith really worried Jesus. Jesus was rejected in the one place he should have felt the most welcome. Teens, too, often feel rejected in places where they should feel the most accepted.

We may not have dramatic healings like the lepers to give thanks for. We may feel welcome and accepted in our "hometown." But we can fail to offer thanks to God for the small miracles that are part of everyday living. It is easier to gripe than to be grateful. Many young people take blessings from God for granted—food, shelter, material comforts, family, friends, and even God's great love. This session is a reminder for them that "it is good to give thanks to the LORD" (Psalm 92:1).

Schedule at a Glance

Session Activities (Total session time: 90 minutes)

A. **Introduction and Opening Prayer** (5 minutes)

B. **From A to Z** (10 minutes), a small-group activity identifying God's gifts

C. **Getting Others Relay** (15 minutes), a large-group activity focusing on saying thanks to God

D. **Circles of Rejection** (20 minutes), a small-group activity on rejection

E. **Snack Break** (10 minutes)

F. **Saying Thank-You to God** (15 minutes), a small-group activity on God's gifts

G. **Prayers in a Bag** (15 minutes), a large-group prayer saying thanks to God

Materials Needed

This is a list of materials needed for all the activities in this session, except the optional activity:

- ☐ blank thank-you notes with envelopes, one for each person
- ☐ Bibles, one for each person
- ☐ pens or pencils
- ☐ sheets of newsprint, one for each small group
- ☐ masking tape
- ☐ several pairs of scissors
- ☐ blue, red, and yellow construction paper
- ☐ copies of handout 4–A, "Circles of Rejection," one for each person
- ☐ snacks
- ☐ four or eight pieces of poster board, depending on your group size
- ☐ markers
- ☐ slips of paper, one for each person
- ☐ a small paper bag

Other Necessary Preparations

- ☐ *For activity C.* Map out a clear area in a gym, the parish hall, or, even better, outside for the relay game. Make sure it is free of tripping hazards.
- ☐ *For activity D.* Cut out circles (about 3 inches or more in diameter) from blue, red, and yellow construction paper. Cut out enough circles so that every participant will have one, but for every six blue circles that you make, cut out only one red and one yellow circle.
- ☐ *For activity F.* Draw in capital block letters on poster board the letters in the word *thank-you.* Use a whole piece of poster board for each letter if you expect to have more than two people working on a letter (more than sixteen participants), otherwise a half piece for each letter will work fine.
- ☐ Review the optional activity at the end of this session and consider whether you would like to use it in some way, for example, in place of another activity, as a way to extend the session, or as a follow-up activity.

Session Activities

Activity A

Introduction and Opening Prayer (5 minutes)

Materials needed. blank thank-you notes with envelopes, one for each person

1. Young people frequently hear from adults what a burden or problem they are. Begin the session by letting them know what a blessing they are to you and to the parish or school community. You may want to do this by reading them a thank-you note, but most important, you should affirm them as a group as well as recognize their unique gifts and talents.

2. Then talk briefly about how we approach God in prayer. Often we go to God only when we want to ask for something. This session is a chance to appreciate all God's blessings and come to God with a spirit of genuine thanksgiving.

Next invite them to complete the following sentence starter with a word or a phrase: "I am thankful for . . ." Invite them to share their prayer in groups of eight to ten people.

When your short opening prayer is over, give everyone a blank thank-you note and tell them that by the time the session is over, it will be up to each individual to decide what to do with it.

Activity B — From A to Z (10 minutes)

Related Scripture passage. Psalm 92

Materials needed. a Bible; pens or pencils; sheets of newsprint, one for each small group

1. Relate this activity to the opening prayer by reading excerpts of Psalm 92. Comment that we must first recognize and appreciate our blessings before we can offer thanks.

2. Form the participants into small groups of five to eight people. Pass out pens or pencils to everyone and give each small group a sheet of newsprint. Direct the groups to write the letters *A* through *M* down the left side of their newsprint and the letters *N* through *Z* down the middle, making two columns.

Tell the young people that when you say, "Go," they are to think of as many things as possible that are gifts from God and try to list by each letter a gift from God that starts with that letter of the alphabet.

3. After about 5 minutes, call time and ask each group how many letters it used. Affirm every group's effort. Follow this by introducing the theme of the session as "Being Thankful." Remind the young people that Christian faith calls believers to be thankful for all God's gifts. Ask them to keep in mind the gifts they identified, as they move on to other activities.

Activity C — Getting Others Relay (15 minutes)

Related Scripture passage. Luke 17:11–16

Materials needed. Bibles, one for each person; masking tape

Before the session. Map out a clear area in a gym, the parish hall, or, even better, outside for the relay game. Make sure it is free of tripping hazards.

1. Ask the participants to turn to Luke 17:11–16 in their Bible and follow along as you read the parable of the ten lepers. Ask them to keep this passage in mind during this activity.

2. Assemble the young people in the spot you chose for the relay. Divide them into teams of five to ten and have the team members line up behind one another, relay style. At the opposite side of the relay area, lay a masking tape line to mark where the young people should run to.

3. Give the following directions for the relay:
- The first person in each line must run to the tape line on the floor, step on it, and return to the starting point. When that person comes back, he or she grabs the hand of the second person in line and they both run up to the tape line, step on it, and return. The third time, three people run up and back, and so on, until every team member has run up and back.

  This is the most important rule: Runners must hold one another's hands the entire time they are running. If they break the link, they need to start that leg of the race over again. No matter which team finishes first, all the teams must keep going until they complete the relay.

4. Give the signal to start the relay. When all the teams have finished, gather the young people together in a large group again. After they catch their breath, reread Luke 17:11–16 and ask the participants what they learned from the game and from the reading. Use the following questions for discussion:
- How is the relay similar to the story of the ten lepers? How is it different?
- Why did only one leper return to say thank-you to Jesus?
- In the relay why was it important to keep going back to get everyone on your team? How is this similar to the way Christian communities should be?
- How do we as a community say, "Thanks," to God?
- Why is the Eucharist often called a sacrament of thanksgiving?

5. Conclude by making the following points in your own words:
- Jesus praises the faith of the one leper who came back to say thank-you and who praised God for his healing. The story teaches us that having faith in God also means having a grateful heart.
- The lepers who did not return to thank Jesus may have felt that they didn't need to say thank-you because of all the suffering they experienced. The story teaches us that even when we experience suffering, we should be grateful for the good things and the gifts that come our way.
- We need to help one another see the good things God has given us. We do this by example when we show our gratitude toward God and other people. It is why we need to give thanks to God as a community.

Activity D Circles of Rejection (20 minutes)

Related Scripture passage. Mark 6:1–6

Materials needed. a pair of scissors; blue, red, and yellow construction paper; pens or pencils; copies of handout 4–A, "Circles of Rejection," one for each person; a Bible

Before the session. Cut out circles (about 3 inches or more in diameter) from blue, red, and yellow construction paper. Cut out enough circles so that every participant will have one, but for every six blue circles that you make, cut out only one red and one yellow circle.

1. Randomly hand out to the young people the colored circles that you created before the session. Tell them that you are going to play a game according to the following directions:

- If you have a blue circle, gather together in a circle with two or three other people who have a blue circle, lock arms with them, and do not allow anyone else to enter your group—no matter what they say or do.
- If you have a red circle, do and say whatever you can to try and gain entry into one of the circles.
- If you have a yellow circle, do not bother trying to enter a circle. Do not show even the slightest interest in joining, no matter what people with red or blue circles may say to you.

2. Begin the game. After about 5 minutes, tell the young people to discard their circle and their role. Pass out pens or pencils and handout 4–A, "Circles of Rejection." Tell the young people to complete the sentence starters in the circles that are labeled with the color of the circle they had. When they finish, invite them to share some of their responses with the whole group.

3. Close this activity by reading aloud Mark 6:1–6 and making the following points:

- We all feel left out and rejected sometimes—just like the lepers were rejected by society and Jesus was rejected in his own hometown.
- Let's all make an effort to be more welcoming and inclusive of others, especially those who may seem—at first—different from us.

Activity E Snack Break (10 minutes)

Activity F Saying Thank-You to God (15 minutes)

Related Scripture passage. Luke 17:11–16

Materials needed. four or eight sheets of poster board, several pairs of scissors, markers

Before the session. Draw in capital block letters on poster board the letters in the word *thank-you.* Use a whole piece of poster board for each letter if you expect to have more than two people working on a letter (more than sixteen participants), otherwise a half piece for each letter will work fine.

1. Introduce this activity in these or similar words:

- Remember the story from the Gospel of Luke we read earlier about the ten lepers who were healed by Jesus. Today, like the one leper who returned to thank Jesus, we have a chance to say thank-you by sending a greeting card to God. But you won't have to go to the card store because this greeting card is made with giant letters that we will hang up to share with the entire parish.

2. If you have sixteen or more participants, divide the young people into eight small groups, making sure each group has at least two people. Give each small group a pair of scissors and one of the sheets of poster board that you prepared before the session. If you have fewer than sixteen participants, make fewer than eight groups and give some groups more than one sheet of poster board.

Direct each small group to cut out its letter and throw away the scraps. Ask everyone to think of things in their life to thank God for—friends, family, nature, their gifts and talents, and so on—and to write these things on their poster board letter with markers. Urge them to come up with as many different things as possible. Remind them that their work is going to be on display so they should write neatly, making the letter look as nice as they can.

3. When they have finished, collect the letters and explain that you will hang the letters in a prominent place in the gathering space of your school or parish, spelling out *thank-you.* Have the young people invite their family and friends to come and add to the posters so that this activity can be a community project as well.

Activity G — Prayers in a Bag (15 minutes)

Materials needed. slips of paper, one for each person; pens or pencils, one for each person; a small paper bag

1. Introduce this prayer activity in these or similar words:

- Our session has focused on the ten lepers and how only one came back to say thank-you to Jesus. We have talked about how it feels to be rejected like the lepers. We saw how Jesus praised the leper who even though rejected by society still had a grateful heart. And as a group, we have listed things we are thankful for.

  In our prayer we often ask God for things. Dear God, give me this, give me that. But we rarely remember to offer thanksgiving prayers. So let us close our session by taking time to do that now.

2. Give each person a slip of paper and a pen or pencil. Direct everyone to write a short thank-you prayer to God, beginning with "Dear God, thank-you for . . ." One sentence is fine, and they should write neatly so that someone else can read it.

3. Collect all the prayers in a small paper bag. You might want to ask another leader to look them over as they are collected to make sure each one is readable and appropriate. Then ask the young people to be quiet as you invite them one at a time to select a prayer from the bag and read it aloud. After each prayer is read, invite the group to respond, "Thank-you, God."

Optional Activity

Servant-Leader Appreciation

Related Scripture passage. Philippians 1:3–6

1. Read or have one of the young people read Philippians 1:3–6. Talk about how important it is to express our thankfulness to the people who give of themselves for us. Ask them to choose someone in their parish or community who gives selflessly to others—somebody whom they would like to recognize and whom they could honestly apply the prayer from Philippians to. He or she may be the pastor or DRE, a volunteer usher, the school custodian, the band director, a coach, and so on.

2. Invite the participants to choose one of the following options for expressing their thankfulness to that person. Be open to other creative thankful options offered by the young people.

- Make a paper chain and write different words of thanks on each link.
- Make a top 10 list of all the great things you appreciate about this person.
- Tape record messages or greetings of thanksgiving for the person to play on her or his car tape player or home stereo.
- Decorate prayer balloons with petitions asking God's blessing on this person.
- Write a prayer or a poem or a newspaper article singing this person's praises.

3. Encourage the young people to find ways to express their thankfulness to other important people in their life.

Scripture References

Additional Scripture Passages

Psalm 89. Forever I will sing of the goodness of the Lord.
Matthew 9:9–13. Jesus loves the outcasts.
Psalm 92. Lord, it is good to give thanks to you.
Psalm 107. Give thanks to the Lord for God is good; God's love is everlasting.

Lectionary Readings

Cycle B
Sixth Sunday of Ordinary Time
Fourteenth Sunday of Ordinary time
Nineteenth Sunday of Ordinary Time

Cycle C
Fourth Sunday of Ordinary Time
Twenty-eighth Sunday of Ordinary Time

Session Follow-Up

Family Connection

Invite the young people to spend a week writing or recording everything—big and small—a parent or guardian does for them. They can keep this thank-you log in their room or backpack, but urge them to keep it a secret.

Some daily or weekly sample entries
- doing my laundry
- driving us to a soccer game
- making dinner

Some big-picture sample entries
- making money to support the whole family
- raising me as a Catholic
- saving money for my college education

At the end of the week, invite the young people to write a thank-you letter—not just a note—telling their parent or guardian how much she or he is appreciated.

Circles of Rejection

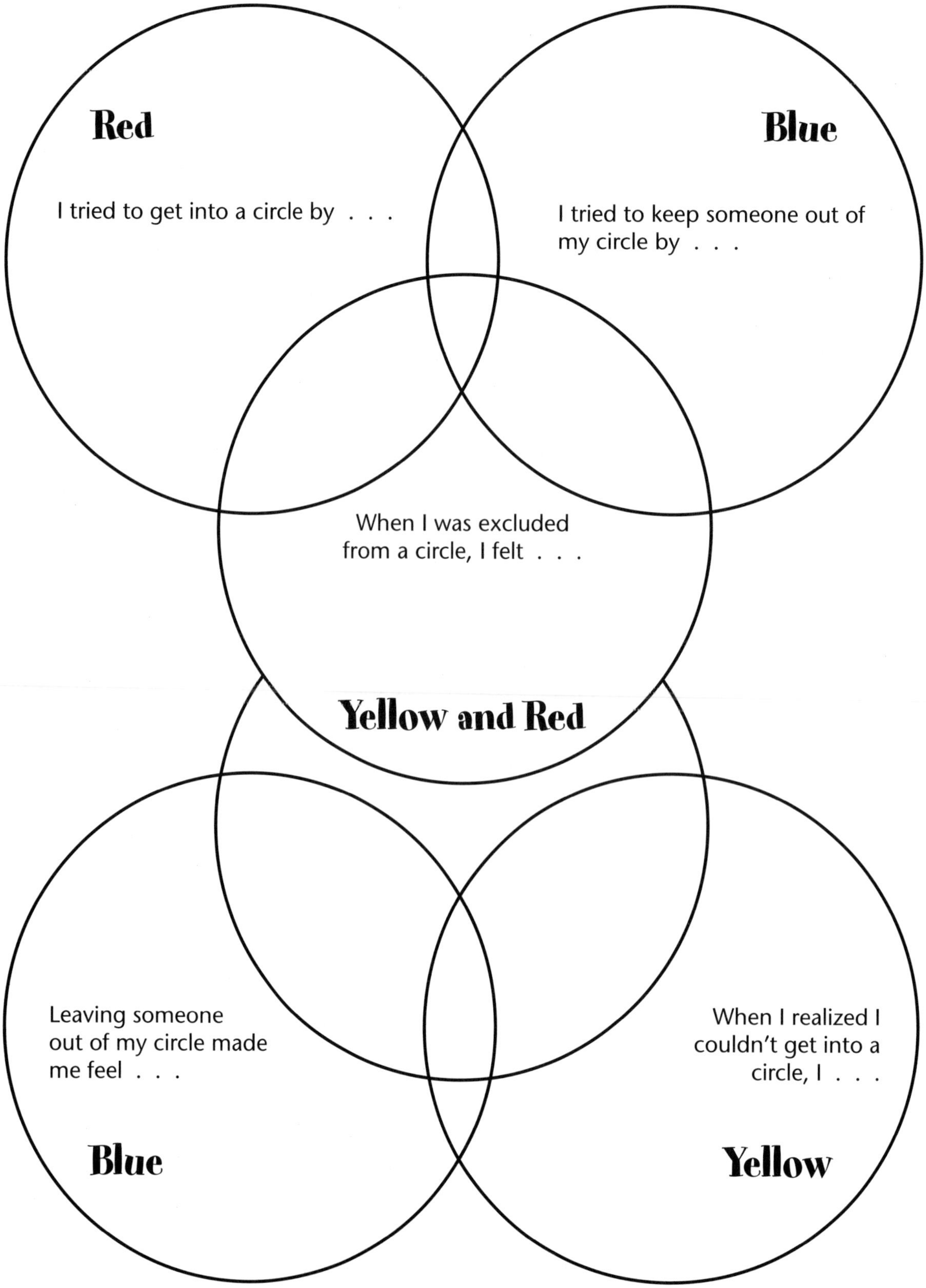
Red
I tried to get into a circle by . . .
Blue
I tried to keep someone out of my circle by . . .
When I was excluded from a circle, I felt . . .
Yellow and Red
Leaving someone out of my circle made me feel . . .
Blue
When I realized I couldn't get into a circle, I . . .
Yellow

Session 5

God's Mercy

Objectives

This session has three objectives:

- To assure the young people of God's loving mercy for each one of them
- To encourage them to examine their conscience and make an effort to change
- To introduce or invite them to pray the stations of the cross

Background on the Session Theme

The central Gospel passage in this session, John 12:20–33, is full of contradictions and seems to have more questions than answers: If you love your life in this world, you will lose it. The Son of Man must die to be glorified. To explain this contradiction, Jesus used the example of a grain of wheat. Just as it seemingly must die and be buried to be reborn as a new plant and bear fruit, Jesus would have to suffer, die, and be resurrected so that we all can be freed from our sins. So too all of us who hope to share in Jesus' new life must die to our selfishness and the evil and sin in our life.

All the readings in this session point to God's incredible love and mercy for each of us. Jeremiah 31:31–34 tells us that God's promises to the Israelites are fulfilled. God not only forgives their evildoing, but wipes the slate clean. "I will . . . remember their sin no more" (verse 34). The reading from Hebrews 5:7–9 reminds us that Jesus, through his obedience and sacrifice, became the source of eternal salvation for all of us.

Teens today need to hear the assurance from Jeremiah that God will never let them down. So many young adolescents have already been disappointed or let down by others in their life—sometimes by so-called friends, even by family members. Some have parents who have divorced; many suffer from promises never kept; all live in a society marred by violence.

In this session the young people are invited to look at their life through the cross and to think about how they can change to respond to Jesus' great love and sacrifice for them. They are called to pray with the psalmist: "Create in me a clean heart, / O God" (Psalm 51:10).

Schedule at a Glance

Session Activities (Total session time: 90 minutes)

A. **Introduction** (5 minutes)

B. **Memory Game** (10 minutes), a small-group icebreaker

C. **Mercy Bags** (15 minutes), a small-group discussion

D. **Drawing on Faith** (20 minutes), a large-group game

E. **Snack Break** (10 minutes)

F. **Bad Habit Charades** (15 minutes), a drama and discussion

G. **Stations of the Cross** (15 minutes), a large-group meditation

Materials Needed

This is a list of materials needed for all the activities in this session, except the optional activity:

- ☐ Bibles, one for each person
- ☐ paper clips, one for each small group
- ☐ paper
- ☐ pens or pencils
- ☐ brown paper lunch bags, one for each small group, to serve as "mercy bags"
- ☐ *contents of each mercy bag:* a button, a rubber band, gold thread, a Lifesaver candy, a tissue, an eraser, a cotton ball, a toothpick, a Band-Aid

- ☐ a flip chart and markers
- ☐ index cards, about forty (more if you want to let the participants write additional cards)
- ☐ envelopes, one for each category used in the game in activity D
- ☐ snacks
- ☐ slips of paper, one for each person
- ☐ a big paper grocery bag
- ☐ a list of the parish's regular times for the sacrament of Reconciliation, and dates of any upcoming parish Reconciliation services, one for each person
- ☐ booklets for praying the stations of the cross, one for each person
- ☐ a pillar candle and matches

Other Necessary Preparations

- ☐ *For activity B.* Make one mercy bag for each small group, putting in each bag the items listed above and closing the bag with a paper clip.
- ☐ *For activity D.* Prepare game cards as directed in activity D.
- ☐ Review the optional activity at the end of this session and consider whether you would like to use it in some way, for example, in place of another activity, as a way to extend the session, or as a follow-up activity.

Session Activities

Activity A

Introduction (5 minutes)

Related Scripture passage. John 12:20–33

1. Ask the young people to step into the shoes of the Apostles Philip and Andrew and listen to today's Gospel through their ears while you proclaim John 12:20–33.

2. You may want to follow up the reading with these comments:

- Pretend you are one of the Apostles. Was Jesus who they expected? Listen to all the contradictions in this Gospel: If you love life, you will lose it; if you want to follow, you will have to serve; if you want to be glorified, you must die. The Apostles must have been wondering what they were getting themselves into.

  Something incredible was about to happen to their savior, Jesus—and it is incredible even for us today. All the Scriptures in this session point to God's incredible mercy and compassion—even to the point of sacrificing God's own Son so our sins would be forgiven.
- How do you think the Apostles responded to Jesus?
- How will you respond to this Gospel?

Activity B Memory Game (10 minutes)

Materials needed. paper clips, one for each small group; paper; pens or pencils; brown paper lunch bags, one for each small group (these will be your mercy bags); items to put in each mercy bag: a button, a rubber band, gold thread, a Lifesaver candy, a tissue, an eraser, a cotton ball, a toothpick, a bandaid

Before the session. Make one mercy bag for each small group, putting in each bag the items listed above and closing the bag with a paper clip.

1. Divide the young people into small groups. Give each group leader a mercy bag but ask everyone not to display the contents of the bag yet.

2. At your signal tell the group leaders to empty the contents of their bag in the center of their group. Do not tell the young people what you are doing.

3. After 1 minute tell the group leaders to quickly put the contents back into the bag. Then give everyone a piece of paper and a pen or a pencil. Direct them to write down from memory all the items they saw.

4. Then tell the young people to compare their list with those of others in their group to see how good each individual's memory is. If no one in their small group remembered all the items, tell the group members to work together to come up with a complete list.

Activity C Mercy Bags (15 minutes)

Related Scripture passage. Jeremiah 31:31–34

Materials needed. mercy bags (see the previous materials needed list), one for each person

1. After playing the memory game in the previous activity, direct each group leader to spread the contents of a mercy bag out in the center of his or her small group again.

2. Invite the young people to read Jeremiah 31:31–34. Share the following comments with the large group:
- In this reading God promises to forgive our sins. God says, "I will be their God, and they shall be my people." In today's activity we are going to talk about the mercy of God.

3. Instruct the young people to look at the items in front of them and to guess what each item might teach us about God's forgiveness and mercy. For example, the rubber band might remind us that God's mercy will always stretch to forgive any sin.

Tell the groups to each choose one person to be the recorder and write down what the group has learned. When they are done with the items in front of them, challenge them to think of at least two other items that might have a message of forgiveness.

4. In the large group, ask item by item what the young people learned about the mercy of God. After you go through all the items in the mercy bag, ask each small group to describe items it came up with on its own.

5. Give each teen a mercy bag to take home as a reminder of God's mercy.

Activity D — Drawing on Faith (20 minutes)

Related Scripture passages. Jeremiah 31:31–34, Psalm 51, Hebrews 5:7–9, John 12:20–33. Note that many of the words and phrases in this activity are drawn from these Scripture passages.

Materials needed. a flip chart and markers; index cards, about forty (more if you want to let the participants write additional cards); envelopes, one for each category used in the game

Before the session. Decide which of the following categories you will use in the game, or make up some of your own. Write each of your chosen words and phrases on a separate index card. Place the index cards for each category in a separate envelope. Prepare at least four categories and responses, one for each of the four readings. If you are using this activity during Lent, add the categories for Lent and Easter, and for Holy Week.

God's name
Father
King
Creator
Jesus
Spirit
Shepherd

Prayer
Scripture
shared prayer
quiet
petition
praise
thanksgiving

Sins needing forgiveness
lying
cheating
stealing
disobeying
hurting oneself
hurting others

Ways to serve others
listening
lending a hand
praying for people
visiting the sick
giving to the poor
feeding the hungry

Symbols of Lent and Easter
a cross
purple
a crown of thorns
the sun
eggs
a butterfly

Holy Week
Palm Sunday
Holy Thursday
Good Friday
Easter Vigil
Easter Sunday

1. Divide the large group of young people into two or three teams. Ask the first team to choose someone to be the first drawer. Present this person with one of your category envelopes and tell her or him to pick a card and quickly draw on the flip chart a picture representing the word or phrase on the card. Numbers, letters, and words are not permitted as clues, and the person drawing is not allowed to speak.

2. The drawer's group has 2 minutes to guess the word or phrase that is being drawn. It has 1 minute to explain how the word relates to the session theme of God's mercy. If the first group cannot guess the drawing or meaning within the time limit, the next group may try.

3. Repeat the process for each card in the category, as time permits. With each new card, alternate the group that gets to draw first.

4. After you do each of the categories prepared ahead of time—and if time permits—you may want to allow each group to write its own list of words or categories for challenging the other teams.

Activity E Snack Break (10 minutes)

Activity F Bad Habit Charades (15 minutes)

Related Scripture passage. Psalm 51

Materials needed. slips of paper, one for each person; a big paper grocery bag; pencils; a list of the parish's regular times for the sacrament of Reconciliation, and dates of any upcoming parish Reconciliation services, one for each person

1. Introduce this activity with comments like the following:

- In Psalm 51 we pray: "Cleanse me from my sin. . . . / Create in me a clean heart." (verses 2–10). It is important that we take a look at our bad habits, the things we need to change about ourselves, and take action to change. Lent, especially, is a great time of year to do some spring cleaning of our heart, but anytime is a good time.

2. Give everyone a slip of paper and a pen or pencil. Ask them to write down a bad habit that either they need to change or that others need to change. It does not have to be personal. Give a couple examples, such as gossiping about others or punching a brother. Put all the slips into a big grocery bag, but look them over to make sure they are appropriate for charades and to avoid duplication.

3. One by one, ask the participants to pick a slip out of the bag. Give them 1 minute to act out the bad habit written on the slip they selected. They may not speak at all during their charade. Encourage the group to guess the habit being acted out. After someone guesses the habit, discuss some positive ways we can try to avoid this type of behavior.

4. Close by encouraging the young people to continue this examination of conscience on their own. Give them a slip of paper listing the regular times when the sacrament of Reconciliation is available at your parish and the dates of any upcoming parish Reconciliation services.

Activity G — Stations of the Cross (15 minutes)

Related Scripture passages. Hebrews 5:7–9, John 12:20–33

Materials needed. booklets for praying the stations of the cross, one for each person (if possible use one written for young people, such as *Stations for Teens: Meditations on the Death and Resurrection of Jesus,* by Gary Egeberg [Winona, MN: Saint Mary's Press, 1999]); a pillar candle and matches

1. Distribute books for praying the stations of the cross and introduce this stations meditation as follows:

- The stations of the cross is a beautiful Catholic tradition that invites us to walk the way of the cross with Jesus and reflect on how his passion teaches us to live daily.

2. Ask for volunteers to do the readings for each station. You'll need one person for each station. Give the readers a few moments to go to their assigned station with their reading and sit down. Designate another teen to be the candle bearer. This teen will move from station to station and stand under the appropriate station during the prayers. Ask the teen sitting at each station to do the reading for that station.

3. After praying the stations together, invite the young people to attend the stations of the cross with the entire community the next time it is scheduled at your parish.

Note: If you do not have time to pray all the stations, pray as many as you have time for.

Optional Activity — Reflecting on the Cross (20 minutes)

This activity would work well after the young people have had an opportunity to pray the stations of the cross together. It can be used immediately following the stations or perhaps it can be used a week later or as a take-home follow-up activity.

Related Scripture passages. Hebrews 5:7–9, John 12:20–33

Materials needed. a list of all fifteen stations of the cross, paper, pens or pencils

Before the session. Make photocopies of the following list of the stations of the cross:

1. Jesus is condemned to death.
2. Jesus accepts the cross.
3. Jesus falls the first time.
4. Jesus meets his mother.

5. Simon helps Jesus carry the cross.
6. Veronica wipes Jesus' face.
7. Jesus falls the second time.
8. Jesus consoles the women.
9. Jesus falls the third time.
10. Jesus is stripped of his garments.
11. Jesus is nailed to the cross.
12. Jesus dies on the cross.
13. Jesus is taken down from the cross.
14. Jesus is buried in the tomb.
15. Jesus rises from the dead.

1. Give each teen a list of the stations of the cross, a pen or pencil, and a sheet of paper. Instruct the young people to spread out in a large area where they can each have some quiet space to reflect and write.

2. Tell the young people to choose one of the fifteen stations, reflect on how it relates to their own life, and write three questions for an examination of conscience and a prayer.

3. Collect and compile these examinations and prayers into a Lenten reflection booklet. It can be redistributed to the young people as a journal reflection throughout the season of Lent, or perhaps shared with the parish community, if the young people agree to share their reflections in this way.

Scripture References

Additional Scripture Passages

Psalm 103. God loves us with mercy.
Psalm 130. God forgives our sins.
Matthew 16:21–27. Jesus predicts his death.
Matthew 26:14–27. The Passion of Jesus
John 3:16–18. The greatest love story
Colossians 1:24–28. Suffer with Christ.
Ephesians 2:4–10. God is always merciful.
2 Timothy 1:8–10. Jesus will defeat death.

Lectionary Readings

Cycle A
Fifth Sunday of Lent
Palm or Passion Sunday
Trinity Sunday
Twenty-second Sunday of Ordinary Time

Cycle B
Fifth Sunday of Lent
Palm or Passion Sunday
Seventh Sunday of Ordinary Time

Cycle C
Palm or Passion Sunday
Seventh Sunday of Ordinary Time

Session Follow-Up

Family Connection

Suggest to the young people that they try the following activity at home. Make copies of the directions to send home with them, along with a copy of the book *Stations for Teens: Meditations on the Death and Resurrection of Jesus,* by Gary Egeberg.

> Pray with your family the meditations in the book *Stations for Teens: Meditations on the Death and Resurrection of Jesus,* by Gary Egeberg. You might want to pray one station of the cross each night for two weeks, allowing time each night for family members to share how the station speaks to them in their own life. Then let them offer any prayers inspired by that station.
>
> At the end of the two weeks, discuss the following question:
>
> - Which station touched you the most? That is, which station speaks the most to you in your life right now?
>
> If your parish holds regular stations of the cross during Lent, attend as a family and join your prayer together with the rest of the community. Your reflection on the stations as a family will give the community celebration even greater meaning. Many parishes are letting families lead the parish celebration of the stations; maybe your family could even lead the prayer on one occasion.

Session 6

Spiritual Blindness

Objectives

This session has three objectives:

- To help the young people see and appreciate the way God works in their life
- To encourage them to appreciate the gift of sight
- To encourage them to stand up for what they believe

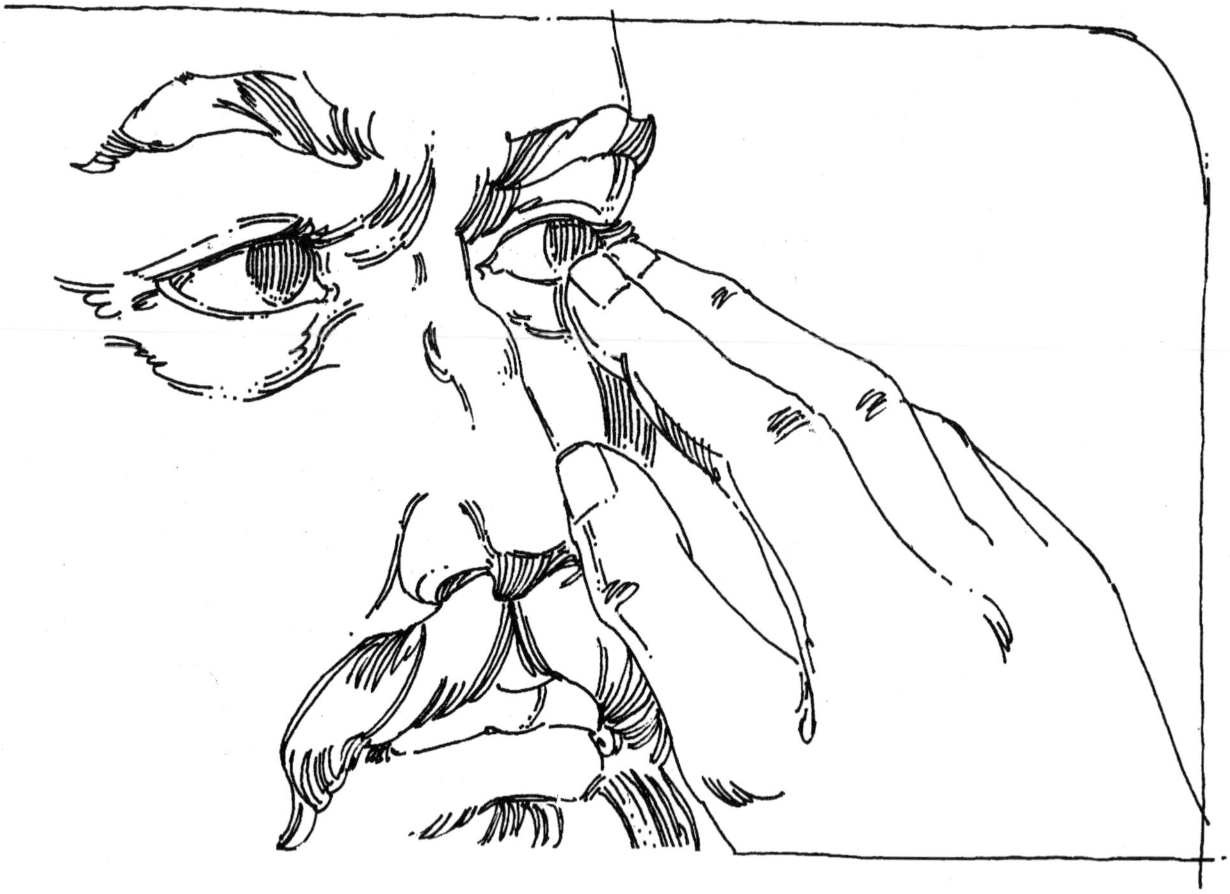

Background on the Session Theme

This session focuses on John 9:1–41, in which Jesus cures a man who was blind from birth. Jesus, the light of the world, enables this man to see with the simple touch of his hands. But after his cure, this man encounters many people who are not able to see God's power. The Pharisees challenge the miracle, even trying to get the man's parents to agree it was a hoax. The man insists that Jesus cured him and gets tossed out of the temple for his faith. The doubters can't see that the Son of God is in their midst.

How difficult it can be for us to stand up for what we believe, especially when it is not very popular to be a Christian. Young adolescents face some tough choices. They feel peer pressure to act a certain way. But this causes spiritual blindness. We need to affirm them to have the courage to live as Jesus wants us to live. They must learn to turn peer pressure around and use it in a positive way—to support and encourage one another.

Schedule at a Glance

Session Activities (Total session time: 90 minutes)

A. **Introduction and Opening Prayer** (5 minutes)

B. **The Caterpillar Game** (20 minutes), a large-group icebreaker on the gift of sight

C. **See How God Is Working in Our Life** (25 minutes), a small-group craft activity

D. **Snack Break** (10 minutes)

E. **Stand Up for What You Believe** (15 minutes), a small-group activity using forced-choice questions

F. **Guided Meditation** (15 minutes), a large-group prayer

Materials Needed

This is a list of materials needed for all the activities in this session, except the optional activity:

- ☐ newsprint and a marker
- ☐ Bibles, one for each person
- ☐ blindfolds, one for each small-group member except the designated guide
- ☐ copies of handout 6–A, "Eyeglasses Mobile," using 8½-by-11-inch pieces of construction paper or card stock, one for each person
- ☐ magazines
- ☐ several pairs of scissors
- ☐ several glue sticks or bottles of glue
- ☐ hole punchers
- ☐ yarn, 1 to 2 feet for each person
- ☐ snacks
- ☐ masking tape
- ☐ pens or pencils
- ☐ copies of handout 6–B, "Stand Up for What You Believe," one for each person

Other Necessary Preparations

- ☐ *For activity B.* Scout out an area outdoors or a big indoor gym or open space for this activity. Choose a route for the "caterpillar" in this activity to travel. Make sure the area is free of obstacles.
- ☐ *For activity E.* Write on a sheet of newsprint the questions listed in activity E. Post the sheet in the meeting room.
- ☐ *For activity F.* Read over the guided meditation script in activity F so that you are comfortable reading it aloud slowly and thoughtfully.
- ☐ Review the optional activity at the end of this session and consider whether you would like to use it in some way, for example, in place of another activity, as a way to extend the session, or as a follow-up activity.

Session Activities

Activity A

Introduction and Opening Prayer (5 minutes)

Related Scripture passage. John 9:1–41

Materials needed. Bibles, one for each person

1. Introduce the session in the following way:

- When we were little, many of us played games to learn about our senses—seeing, hearing, smelling, touching, and tasting.

  We tasted lemons to learn what is sour and tasted chocolate to know what is sweet. We listened to different sounds to learn the difference between quiet and loud. We put our hand in lunch bags to identify a pine cone or a cotton ball by touch. Very early we learned to smile at the sight of a loved one. And later we got hungry at the smell of popcorn.

  It is easy to take our senses for granted, just as we rarely think about the air we breathe or the way our heart beats. But what would you do if the world suddenly became dark? suddenly quiet? What would you do if you could not taste or smell or touch anything?

2. Read John 9:1–41 aloud and invite the participants to follow along in their Bible. When you are finished, tell them that in this session they will celebrate the gift of sight and what it takes to see and believe.

3. Finish by praying:

- Lord, help us always to be aware that our senses are a gift from you.
  Lord, help us to see your goodness,
  hear your goodness,
  taste your goodness,
  touch your goodness,
  smell your goodness
  in our everyday lives.
  Amen.

Activity B — The Caterpillar Game (20 minutes)

Materials needed. blindfolds, one for each small-group member except the designated guide

Before the session. Scout out an area outdoors or a big indoor gym or open space for this activity. Choose a route for the "caterpillar" in this activity to travel. Make sure the area is free of obstacles.

1. Divide the participants into small groups of eight to ten people. Designate one person in each group as the guide. Brief the guides on the route the caterpillars are to travel. Give everyone else a blindfold and tell them to put it on.

Line up the blindfolded participants of each small group single file, so if you have three small groups, you will have three short single-file lines. Direct the people in the lines to place their hands on the shoulders of the person in front of them.

2. Tell the guides to begin directing their caterpillar on how to travel a designated route. The guides may only speak; they may not guide a caterpillar by, for example, taking the hand of the person at the front of the line.

If time permits, the groups may switch their person giving directions with one of the blindfolded group members.

3. After you have given the groups a few minutes to navigate the course, gather everyone together and discuss the following questions:

- What did you learn from this activity about sight?
- What did you learn about trust?
- What did you learn about God?

Conclude this activity by thanking God for the gift of sight and for helping us to see even when we are temporarily blinded from doing what is right. Encourage the young people to guide one another and to be a positive force when they see someone going astray.

Activity C — See How God Is Working in Our Life (25 minutes)

Related Scripture passage. John 9:1–41

Materials needed. copies of handout 6–A, "Eyeglasses Mobile," using 8½-by-11-inch pieces of construction paper or card stock, one for each person; magazines; several pairs of scissors; several glue sticks or bottles of glue; hole punchers; yarn, 1 to 2 feet for each person

1. Introduce this activity with words like the following:

- In the Gospel of John [9:1–41], Jesus gives a blind man his sight so that he is able to see clearly how God is working in his life. By proclaiming to others what Jesus has done, the blind man is able to show them more clearly what God has done.

  During this activity you have a chance to recognize the many good ways God is working in your life and to share those good things with the rest of the parish so that they can better see all the good God has done for us.

2. Direct the young people to regather into their caterpillar groups. Give each teen a copy of handout 6–A on construction paper or card stock. Distribute scissors, glue sticks or bottles of glue, and magazines to each small group. Direct the young people to fill in each lens of the eyeglasses with words or pictures of some of the good things God has done for us. Tell them to cut out their words and pictures from the magazines that you have provided and glue them in place. Give examples such as the following to get them started:

- A photo of a parent and child could be used to illustrate the gift of family.
- The word *friends* could be pasted in to show appreciation for the gift of friendship.

3. When everyone has filled in their lenses, direct them to cut out their eyeglasses along the dotted line, punch a hole in the top, and tie a 1- to 2-foot piece of yarn through it. Tell the young people that you will hang the eyeglasses somewhere in the parish or school.

Conclude this activity by urging the young people to open their eyes in their everyday life so that they can better see God's goodness all around them.

Activity D Snack Break (10 minutes)

Activity E Stand Up for What You Believe (15 minutes)

Related Scripture passage. John 9:1–41

Materials needed. newsprint and a marker; masking tape; pens or pencils; copies of handout 6–B, "Stand Up for What You Believe," one for each person

Before the session. Write the following questions on a sheet of newsprint and post it in the meeting room:

- Why was it a difficult choice?
- What are some of the pressures you feel about making a choice?
- What supports you in making a right choice?
- What choice is Jesus calling you to make?
- What can you do to start moving toward the right choice?

1. Introduce this activity with words like the following:

- After the blind man is healed [John 9:1–41], the Pharisees and the Jews ask him several times to explain what has happened to him. He is required to witness to others about the miracle that God has given him in restoring his sight—he has to stand up for what he believes. And doing so comes with a price—he eventually gets tossed out of the Temple for witnessing about Jesus Christ.

We too must witness with our words and actions of what it means to be a follower of Christ. Jesus has opened our eyes to see what is right and wrong, and this knowledge often forces us to make some tough choices.

2. Give everyone a pen or pencil and a copy of handout 6–B, "Stand Up for What You Believe." Direct them to find a comfortable place to complete the handout quietly on their own. Urge them to make their choices as honestly as possible.

3. Have the participants gather into their small groups and direct them to pick one handout question to talk about with the rest of their group. After they each share how they responded to the forced-choice question, suggest that they explore the topic further with the discussion questions that you posted before the session.

Do not force anyone to talk about a topic if they are uncomfortable doing so, but encourage them to talk a little about at least one question.

Activity F Guided Meditation (15 minutes)

Related Scripture passage. The meditation that follows was inspired by Luke 2:41–50.

Before the session. Read over the following guided meditation script so that you are comfortable reading it aloud slowly and thoughtfully.

1. Ask the young people to spread out in a comfortable space—preferably on a carpeted floor—and give one another space. Suggest that they choose any position that they find comfortable.

2. Set the tone for the meditation by dimming the lights and lighting a candle. Guide the young people through the following meditation by reading it aloud slowly and thoughtfully. Pause where you see ellipses (. . .).

- Close your eyes. . . . In your mind go to your favorite place where you can be alone . . . and safe . . . all alone and very safe. . . . Look around at the familiar things. . . . Each item you see brings to mind a happy memory . . . a memory of a time that was good . . . a time of contentment . . . a happy memory when you were young and playful . . . when you were curious . . . when you were free. . . .

  Close your eyes tighter . . . and feel the warmth of those memories . . . feel the warmth of a friendship . . . of someone who cares about you and knows you better than you know yourself. . . . Stand with your eyes closed and feel a new friend coming up behind you. . . . Know that you are safe and the friend will protect you. . . . From behind you . . . feel the warmth of his love . . . the depth of his caring . . . his gentle playfulness. . . .

From behind . . . he gently cups his hands over your eyes like a playful friend. . . . He gently laughs and, like a special friend who has missed you, he gives you a hug. . . . He turns you around, and you can look up and see the smiling face of a teenager . . . of Jesus . . . Jesus when he was a teenager. . . . Look at his youthful eyes that sparkle . . . eyes that look right into you . . . deeply . . . knowing your joys as well as your hurts . . . eyes that can see beyond any walls you may have built . . . walls that were to protect . . . walls that now melt. . . .

Look into the gentle eyes of a Jesus who understands so well . . . and can see the beauty in you that has been hidden. . . . Listen to the Lord thank you for inviting him to be with you. . . . He has come to you in your favorite place . . . so now he takes you to his favorite place . . . where he feels very much at home. . . .

The Lord takes your hand . . . and you feel secure. . . . He takes you to a building . . . a place of worship . . . a house of prayer. . . . What does the place of worship look like to you? . . . Is it large? . . . small? . . . bright? . . . dim? . . . And he tells you of a time when he met the ancient ones here . . . people of great wisdom. . . . Here is where he discovered who he was . . . and found strength to begin his destiny . . . his task. . . . And those teachers shared their gifts with him . . . their talents. . . . They encouraged him. . . . They helped him become free.

Now it is your turn . . . and Jesus promises that he will stay close to you . . . to show you . . . to help you. . . . Is there anything you want to say to Jesus? . . . Anything you want to do? . . .

Jesus now stands before you. . . . He quietly asks you to close your eyes. . . . He raises his hands and softly places his fingers over your closed eyelids . . . gently rubbing them as if he were pushing away the pressure . . . the tension. . . .

He tells you that you are free . . . there will be no more expectations . . . no more demands . . . no more pressure. . . . Just be who you are . . . and be loved as you are . . . without all the expectations. . . . Nothing is required . . . nothing is called for. . . .

And you can feel the miraculous touch of Jesus as he seems to rub away the darkness from your closed eyes. . . . You can see yourself years from now . . . in a new way . . . fulfilling God's will . . . fulfilling God's plan . . . becoming the person you dream of . . . the person that God hopes you will be someday. . . .

Be at peace . . . and be filled with delight. . . . With your eyes closed, . . . how do you see yourself? . . . What is that person like . . . the you that is yet to come? . . . Is there anything you would like to ask that person? anything you would like to say? . . .

Be at peace. . . . Jesus promises that he will always be there for you as you grow and become the person you are meant to be. . . . He will always be standing near you . . . waiting for you to ask for his help. . . . And if you ask him . . . he promises to help you fulfill the dream . . . to become all that God created you to be. . . .

Be at peace. . . . Know that the Lord is so near to you . . . ready to help if only you ask. . . .

Be at peace. . . . (Based on Thomas F. Catucci, *Time with Jesus,* pages 33–38)

Optional Activity

The Magic Eye—God Sees Differently Than We See (20 minutes)

Related Scripture passage. 1 Samuel 16:1–13

Materials needed. a Bible; Magic Eye puzzles, one for each small group (These often can be found in the comic section of Sunday newspapers. Also, Magic Eye books are available at many libraries.); copies of the discussion questions in step 3 below, one for each small group

1. Introduce the Scripture reading:

- Listen to this reading from Samuel and the conversation he has with the Lord. He says: "Not as man sees does God see, because man sees the appearance but the Lord looks into the heart" (1 Samuel 16:7).

Read aloud 1 Samuel 16:1–13.

Explain to the group members that in this activity, they will be asked to look at some pictures and see if they can find the hidden messages in them. Afterward they will discuss in their small group some questions about the way we see things and how different it is from the way God sees things.

2. Divide the participants into groups of seven to eight people each. Give each group a Magic Eye picture. Tell the young people to pass it around their group and see if everyone can find the hidden picture. Allow each teen a few minutes to study the picture. Most likely some of them will be able to see the picture right away, and others may take awhile.

3. After everyone has had a chance to look at the Magic Eye picture, distribute a copy of the following discussion questions to each group. Give everyone a few minutes to answer them in their small groups.

- Do we all see things in the same way? Why or why not?
- Do we sometimes look at things without really seeing them?
- When we first meet someone, how do we usually see them?
- After we get to know them, how do they look different to us?
- How do you think God looks at you as compared with how other people see you?
- What do you think it means when the Scriptures say, "the Lord looks into the heart" (1 Samuel 16:7)?

Close by asking the participants to quietly reflect on what God sees when God looks into their heart.

Scripture References

Additional Scripture Passages

Isaiah 9:1 or 9:2. Light in the darkness
Isaiah 35:4–7. The eyes of the blind will be opened.
Mark 7:31–37. Making the deaf hear
Isaiah 42:1–4,6–7. A light for the nations
Psalm 34:8. Taste and see the goodness of the Lord.

Lectionary Readings

Cycle A
Fourth Sunday of Lent

Cycle B
Fourth Sunday of Lent
Twenty-third Sunday of Ordinary Time

Session Follow-Up

Family Connection

Suggest to the young people that they try the following activity at home. Make copies of the directions to send home with them. And purchase some inexpensive cardboard kaleidoscopes from a dollar store and send one home with each young person.

> Let each family member look through a kaleidoscope and describe what he or she sees. We all look through the same kaleidoscope, but we see different things. Similarly, we are all part of one family, but we see things differently, through different eyes.
>
> From looking through a kaleidoscope, what can we learn about God? about ourselves? about the gift of sight?
>
> Complete the following sentence-starters and share your responses with one another:
>
> - I see God in myself when . . .
> - I see God in you when . . .

Eyeglasses Mobile

Fill in each lens of the eyeglasses with words or pictures of some of the good things God has done for us. Cut out words and pictures from magazines and glue them in place. Then cut out the eyeglasses along the dotted line, punch a hole in the top, and tie a 1- to 2-foot piece of yarn through it.

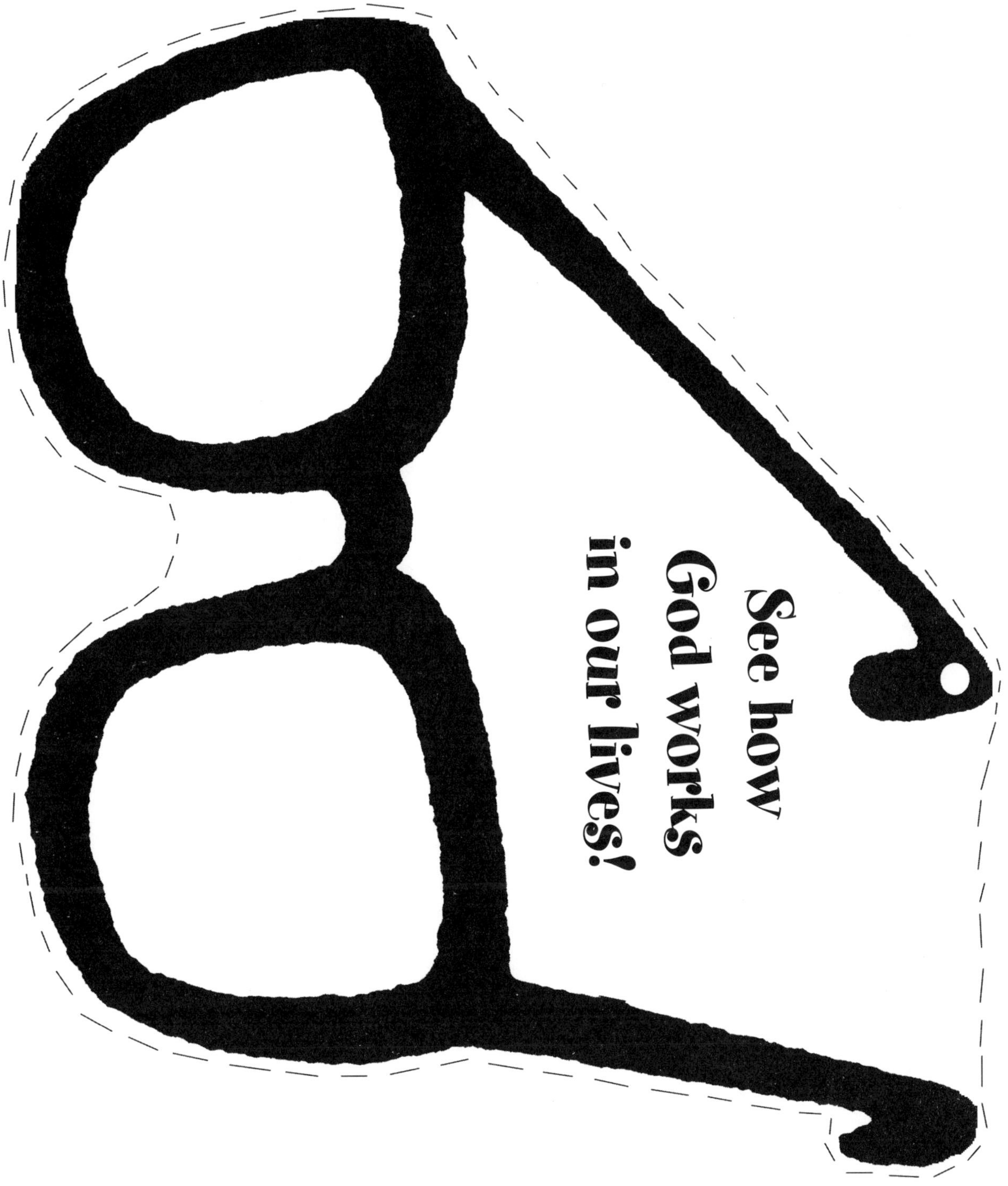
See how
God works
in our lives!

Stand Up for What You Believe

For each choice below, circle the portion of each question that reflects how you would be more likely to act.

Are you more likely to . . .

do what your friends say	or	do what your parents say
do what you know is right	or	do what you feel like doing
go to Mass because your parents make you go	or	go to Mass and try to get something out of it
share your faith in God	or	just make jokes about it
do things to help out	or	wait to be nagged
admit when you have done something wrong	or	lie to cover it up
fight violence with violence	or	find a peaceful solution
join cliques to keep new people out	or	help others feel welcome
make fun of others	or	accept their differences
take time to talk to your parents	or	just ignore them
listen to the readings at Mass	or	daydream about what you plan to do later

Session 7

The Spirit's Promise

Objectives

This session has three objectives:

- To help the young people learn more about the Holy Spirit
- To encourage them to recognize and use their gifts from the Holy Spirit
- To encourage them to stop and really think about the words they pray in the creed

Background on the Session Theme

This session can help the young people become familiar with the biblical teaching on the role of the Holy Spirit. The passage from John 14:15–17 is used to introduce the Spirit Hunt icebreaker. It is Jesus' parting words of comfort to his Apostles. Jesus knows they will feel frightened and alone after he ascends to heaven to be with his Father. He promises to send the Holy Spirit to guide and protect them. "I will not leave you orphaned; I am coming to you" (John 14:18).

Paul writes in 1 Corinthians, chapter 12, that it is good to be different and have different gifts. If we were all the same, we would not be able to serve God in all the rich and wonderful ways that make us unique. The Spirit works through each of us so that we can serve others and give glory to God.

In Acts of the Apostles, chapter 2, we read about the birthday of the church—Pentecost—and how the Spirit first came to the Apostles in "a violent wind" (verse 2) and that tongues of fire "rested on each of them" (verse 3). They not only were filled with courage to proclaim the Gospel boldly but were able to witness to God in every language imaginable.

The spirit of God is a mystery to us. Most young people have grown up with God as Father and likely have prayed to Jesus as friend, but it is a lot harder for them to put their arms around the Holy Spirit.

As young people enter junior high school, life gets more complicated and choices become tougher. Sometimes, like the Apostles, they can feel really alone. We need to help young people recognize that the Holy Spirit is a gift from Jesus to each of us to be a comforting presence during those hard and lonely times. The gifts of the Holy Spirit are more than just a list to memorize—they are real helps in our everyday life.

Schedule at a Glance

Session Activities (Total session time: 90 minutes)

A. **Introduction and Opening Prayer** (5 minutes)

B. **Spirit Hunt Icebreaker** (25 minutes), a large-group icebreaker

C. **Gifts of the Holy Spirit** (20 minutes), a small-group activity

D. **Snack Break** (10 minutes)

E. **Piecing Together Our Creed** (20 minutes), a large-group activity on the question What does our creed teach us about the Holy Spirit?

F. **O Great Spirit** (10 minutes), an American Indian prayer

Materials Needed

This is a list of materials needed for all the activities in this session, except the optional activity:

- ☐ Bibles, one for each person
- ☐ seven red candles with holders
- ☐ matches
- ☐ copies of a Spirit Hunt clues handout of your own devising, one for each person
- ☐ pens or pencils
- ☐ large index cards

- ☐ masking tape
- ☐ markers, one for each small group
- ☐ half-sheets of white paper, thirty for each small group
- ☐ newsprint
- ☐ snacks
- ☐ a large sheet of paper
- ☐ a pair of scissors
- ☐ copies of handout 7–A, "The Nicene Creed," one for each person
- ☐ copies of handout 7–B, "O Great Spirit," one for each person

Other Necessary Preparations

- ☐ *For activity A.* Read over the Holy Spirit prayer in step 3 and decide if you will need to substitute the language for the gifts of the Spirit that your group is most familiar with.
- ☐ *For activity B.* Using the sample clues on resource 7–A as a guide, create a handout with a set of clues for the Spirit Hunt. Leave blank space in which the participants can write their answers.
- ☐ *For activity E.* Copy the words of the Nicene Creed (see handout 7–A) onto a large sheet of paper and cut the paper into as many slips as you have participants, with one or more lines of the creed on each piece. Scramble up the slips of paper so that they are in no particular order when you pass them out.
- ☐ Review the optional activity at the end of this session and consider whether you would like to use it in some way, for example, in place of another activity, as a way to extend the session, or as a follow-up activity.

Session Activities

Activity A

Introduction and Opening Prayer (5 minutes)

Related Scripture passage. John 14:15–17

Materials needed. Bibles, one for each person; seven red candles with holders; matches

Before the session. Read over the Holy Spirit prayer in step 3 and decide if you will need to substitute the language for the gifts of the Spirit that your group is most familiar with. Right judgment is often called counsel. Courage is sometimes called fortitude or strength. Reverence is also called piety. More traditional language uses fear of the Lord instead of wonder and awe.

1. Begin your session by inviting the young people to share their answers to the following questions:

- Who is the Holy Spirit?
- Is it tougher to describe the Holy Spirit than to talk about God the Father, or Jesus?

- How many of you pray to God the Father [hint: they pray to God the Father every time they pray the Lord's Prayer], and how often do you pray to Jesus?
- How often do you pray to the Spirit?

Acknowledge that the Spirit remains a mystery of faith for many people, adults as well as youth.

2. Read or have someone else read John 14:15–17. Direct the young people to follow along in their Bible. After reading the passage, address the following questions to the group:

- Why were the Apostles hiding after Jesus ascended to heaven? Why were they afraid?
- After the Holy Spirit came to the Apostles, what were they empowered to do? What did the Spirit give to them?
- Do you have any of the gifts of the Holy Spirit?
- Do you think the Apostles had some of them before the Spirit came?

Tell the young people that the Holy Spirit gives us gifts so that we are able to serve God and others. Explain that during the session today, they will learn more about how to live these gifts and grow in knowledge of the Holy Spirit.

3. Gather the young people around the seven red candles. Ask them to pray silently for the gift of the Spirit they need most in their life right now, as you, or someone you appoint, read the following prayer:

- Come, Holy Spirit, fill us with wisdom. [Light the first candle.]
  Come, Holy Spirit, fill us with understanding. [Light the second candle.]
  Come, Holy Spirit, fill us with right judgment. [Light the third candle.]
  Come, Holy Spirit, fill us with knowledge. [Light the fourth candle.]
  Come, Holy Spirit, fill us with courage. [Light the fifth candle.]
  Come, Holy Spirit, fill us with reverence. [Light the sixth candle.]
  Come, Holy Spirit, fill us with wonder and awe. [Light the seventh candle.] Amen.

Activity B Spirit Hunt Icebreaker (25 minutes)

Related Scripture passage. John 14:15–17

Materials needed. copies of a Spirit Hunt clues handout of your own devising, one for each person; pens or pencils; large index cards; masking tape

Before the session. Using the sample clues on resource 7–A as a guide, create a handout with a set of clues for the Spirit Hunt. Leave blank space in which the participants can write their answers.

Adjust the clues based on your surroundings. Each clue will lead the participants to a corresponding answer card hidden somewhere in or around the building where you meet. When creating your clues, think about the placement of the answer cards. You will want them to be a good distance apart from one another, without making them too easy or too hard to find. For each clue on your handout, create a corresponding answer card on a large index card and tape the card in its hiding spot.

1. Introduce the Spirit Hunt with comments along the following lines:

- We just read from the Gospel of John about the promise of the Holy Spirit as we await Pentecost. Let's find out what you know about the Holy Spirit.

Distribute to each teen a pen or pencil and a copy of the Spirit Hunt handout that you created. Explain to the participants that they will have to do some searching in and around the church or school to fill in all the answers on the handout. Ask them to search for the clues on their own and return to the circle when they are done. Stress that they should leave the answer cards where they find them.

Option. You may want to divide the participants into pairs or teams of three for this activity. If so, have each pair or team start at a different question on the handout so that everyone is not traveling in a pack.

2. When the young people return to the meeting area, go over the following answers together. Encourage them to continue learning more about the Holy Spirit, often the most mysterious and neglected member of the Trinity.

Spirit Hunt answers. The following answers correspond to the sample clues on resource 7–A:

1. Holy Spirit
2. Jesus
3. wisdom, understanding, right judgment, courage, knowledge, reverence, and wonder and awe (See the note on page 75 about using the language for the gifts of the spirit that your group is most familiar with.)
4. Come, Holy Spirit, fill the hearts of your faithful.
And kindle in them the fire of your love.
Send forth your Spirit and they shall be created.
And you shall renew the face of the Earth.
5. Confirmation
6. wind and fire
7. Pentecost
8. John 14:15–17, Acts of the Apostles 2:1–11, 1 Corinthians 12:3–7
9. [your bishop's name]
10. "The Spirit Is a Movin'"

Activity C — Gifts of the Holy Spirit (20 minutes)

Related Scripture passage. 1 Corinthians 12:3–7

Materials needed. Bibles; markers, one for each small group; masking tape; half-sheets of white paper, thirty for each small group; newsprint

1. Divide the group into small groups of six to eight people each. Ask the young people to open their Bible to 1 Corinthians 12:3–7. Read aloud the passage as they follow along. Then give each small group thirty half-sheets of white paper, a marker, and some masking tape.

2. Direct each group to list as many gifts and talents as they can, each on a separate piece of paper. Stress that these must be nonmaterial gifts. Give some examples, such as being a good communicator, being a good listener, being a good sport.

Tell the groups that as they write down the gifts, they should tape the papers end to end. Explain that each group's goal is to have the longest list of gifts at the end of 5 minutes.

3. When time is up, gather all the young people into a circle and pose the following questions:

- What are the gifts of the Holy Spirit? [List them on poster paper as participants name them: wisdom, understanding, right judgment, courage, knowledge, reverence, and wonder and awe.]
- Why do you think the Spirit gives us these gifts? What could we use them for? [Ask the young people to give examples from their own life.]
- How do you think the Spirit helps us to use the gifts you listed on the slips in this last activity?
- Read the Scripture passage 1 Corinthians 12:3–7 silently. What can we learn about our gifts from this passage?

Activity D — Snack Break (10 minutes)

Activity E — Piecing Together Our Creed (20 minutes)

Related Scripture passages. John 14:15–17, Acts of the Apostles 2:1–11, 1 Corinthians 12:3–7

Materials needed. a large sheet of paper; a marker; a pair of scissors; copies of handout 7–A, "The Nicene Creed," one for each person

Before the session. Copy the words of the Nicene Creed (see handout 7–A) onto a large sheet of paper and cut the paper into as many slips as you have young people, with one or more lines of the creed on each piece. Scramble up the slips of paper so that they are in no particular order when you pass them out.

1. Give each teen one of the Nicene Creed puzzle pieces that you prepared before the session. Direct everyone to line up so that the creed is in order from start to finish. Tell them that they will have to work together and read one another's puzzle pieces to do this.

2. When everyone thinks they are standing in the correct place, start at the front of the line and have each person read aloud his or her portion of the creed.

3. Gather everyone together for a brief discussion. Ask,

- What part of the creed tells us about the Holy Spirit?

Direct those who are holding the part of the creed related to the Holy Spirit to read their phrases aloud again, in order.

Ask:

- What does our creed teach us about the Holy Spirit?
- What do we really mean when we pray this prayer every Sunday?

4. Close by encouraging the young people to continue learning more about the Holy Spirit, and give each one a copy of handout 7–A to take home.

(This activity is adapted from Lisa-Marie Calderone-Stewart, *Faith Works for Junior High,* pages 60–64.)

Activity F O Great Spirit (10 minutes)

Related Scripture passage. Acts of the Apostles 2:1–11

Materials needed. copies of handout 7–B, "O Great Spirit," one for each person

1. Begin the closing prayer by leading the group in making the sign of the cross, asking them to pause briefly after naming each member of the Trinity. Then read aloud—or have a group member read aloud—Acts of the Apostles 2:1–11. Share a brief reflection, making the following points:

- In this passage the gift of the Holy Spirit makes it possible for people of different cultures to communicate. It represents a reversal of the divisions between people symbolized by the story about the tower of Babel in the Book of Genesis.
- In the church today, the Holy Spirit helps us hear and appreciate the wisdom of other cultures. This wisdom helps us more deeply appreciate our own beliefs as Christians.
- So just as the Holy Spirit came to the Apostles at Pentecost, we come in prayer asking for courage, wisdom, and understanding—particularly in healing the divisions that exist between peoples and cultures.

2. To close, invite the young people to pray aloud the beautiful American Indian prayer on handout 7–B, "O Great Spirit."

Optional Activity

Giant Word Search (20 minutes)

Materials needed. large sheets of grid paper, one for each small group; markers, a pack for each small group; poster board (optional); masking tape (optional)

Before the session. Copy the word search from resource 7–B, "Spirit Word Search," onto large sheets of grid paper so that each small group will have its own giant word search.

1. Assemble the young people in small groups and give each group a pack of markers and one of the giant word search puzzles that you created before the session. Tell the young people that twenty words about the Holy Spirit are hidden in the word search. Direct them to take turns searching for a word, circling it, and telling their group what the word has to do with the Holy Spirit.

2. When all the groups are finished, gather them in a large group and ask for volunteers to tell which words they found and what they mean. You might want to keep a tally of the words they talk about on a white piece of poster board on the wall.

(This activity is from Maryann Hakowski, *Growing with Jesus,* pages 235–236.)

Scripture References

Additional Scripture Passages

John 16:12–15. The Spirit of truth
Matthew 28:16–20. Baptism in the Spirit
Acts of the Apostles 8:5–17. Conferring the Holy Spirit
John 20:19–23. Receiving the Holy Spirit
Psalm 104. The Lord sends out the Spirit and renews the face of the Earth.
Romans 8:22–27. The Spirit is our hope.
Romans 8:14–17. Led by the Spirit
Romans 5:1–5. Love of God poured out in the Spirit
Acts of the Apostles 5:12–16. The Spirit builds the church.

Lectionary Readings

Cycle A
Sixth Sunday of Easter
Pentecost Sunday

Cycle B
Pentecost Sunday
Trinity Sunday

Cycle C
Sixth Sunday of Easter
Pentecost Sunday
Trinity Sunday

Session Follow-Up

Family Connection

Suggest to the young people that they try the following activity at home. Make copies of the directions to send home with them.

Look up the fruits of the Holy Spirit listed in Galatians 5:22: love, joy, peace, patience, kindness, generosity, faithfulness, gentleness, and self-control. Reflect on the last weekend or week and describe the following experiences:

- a time when one of these gifts came in handy
- a time when you wished you had called upon this gift

Then have each family member choose one gift she or he would like to work on more this week and join in prayer for each person. For example:

- Holy Spirit, please help Ann be more generous in helping her friends with their homework.
- Holy Spirit, please give Dad patience when making tough decisions at work this week.

Each person should put the words of the fruit he or she has chosen in at least two places as visual reminders. Put one sign at home where it will be seen a lot (the bathroom mirror, the refrigerator, a desk) and one in a place that travels with the person (a book bag, a briefcase, a purse). Remember to pray for one another's Spirit intentions as well.

Spirit Hunt Clues

1. For the name of the third person in the Blessed Trinity, look behind the altar.

   ____

2. For the name of God's Son who sends us his spirit, look under a picnic table.

   ____

3. For the seven gifts of the Holy Spirit, look in the nursery.

   ____

   ____

4. For a prayer about the Holy Spirit, look in the library.

   ____

   ____

   ____

5. For the name of the third sacrament of initiation, look near the sliding board.

   ____

6. For the two signs of nature through which the Holy Spirit appeared, look under two tables in the commons.

   ____

7. For the name of the day when the Holy Spirit first appeared to the Apostles, look by the red flame statue outside the church.

   ____

8. For three Bible verses about the Holy Spirit, look in the preschool room.

   ____

9. For the name of the minister of the sacrament of Confirmation, look near the Holy Spirit sign outside.

   ____

10. For the name of a hymn to the Holy Spirit, look by the piano.

   ____

The Nicene Creed

We believe in one God,
the Father, the Almighty,
maker of heaven and earth,
of all that is, seen and unseen.

We believe in one Lord, Jesus Christ,
the only Son of God
eternally begotten of the Father,
God from God, Light from Light,
true God from true God,
begotten, not made, one in Being with the Father.
Through him all things were made.
For us men and for our salvation
he came down from heaven:
by the power of the Holy Spirit
he was born of the Virgin Mary,
and became man.

For our sake he was crucified
under Pontius Pilate;
he suffered, died, and was buried.

On the third day he rose again
in fulfillment of the Scriptures;

he ascended into heaven
and is seated at the right hand of the Father.
He will come again in glory
to judge the living and the dead,
and his kingdom will have no end.

We believe in the Holy Spirit,
the Lord, the giver of life,
who proceeds from the Father and the Son.
With the Father and the Son
he is worshipped and glorified.
He has spoken through the Prophets.
We believe in one holy catholic and apostolic Church.
We acknowledge one baptism for the forgiveness of sins.
We look for the resurrection of the dead,
and the life of the world to come. Amen.

(*Catechism of the Catholic Church,* pages 49–50)

O Great Spirit

O Great Spirit,

Whose voice I hear in the winds,

And whose breath gives life to the world, hear me! I am small and weak.

I need your strength and wisdom.

Let me walk in beauty, and make my eyes ever behold the red and purple sunset.

Make my hands respect the things you have made and my ears sharp to hear your voice.

Make me wise so that I may understand things you have taught my people.

Let me learn the lessons you have hidden in every leaf and rock.

I seek strength, not to be greater than my brother [or sister], but to fight my greatest enemy—myself.

Make me always be ready to come to you with clean hands and straight eyes.

So when life fades, as the fading sunset, my spirit may come to you without shame.

(*A Book of Prayers*)

Spirit Word Search

Copy the following word search onto large sheets of grid paper so that each small group has its own giant word search.

Word list

Confirmation	understanding	sponsor
Pentecost	knowledge	Christian
bishop	courage	faith
community	piety	chrism
celebration	counsel	prayer
service	gifts	reverence
wisdom	sacrament	

C	E	L	E	B	R	A	T	I	O	N	G
T	O	L	S	E	P	G	R	A	T	L	N
R	K	N	O	W	L	E	D	G	E	M	I
O	S	T	F	I	G	A	M	S	T	S	D
S	P	H	T	I	A	F	N	N	L	I	N
N	E	C	K	R	R	U	E	O	R	R	A
O	N	E	E	Y	O	M	V	N	Y	H	T
P	T	C	C	C	A	E	A	E	T	C	S
S	E	L	O	R	N	I	T	T	E	B	R
C	C	I	C	M	T	E	P	L	I	A	E
D	O	A	M	S	M	R	R	S	P	O	D
A	S	U	I	O	A	U	H	E	Y	W	N
D	T	R	R	Y	D	O	N	D	V	N	U
A	H	H	E	A	P	S	N	I	N	E	A
C	A	R	O	W	G	A	I	M	T	R	R
K	E	C	I	V	R	E	S	W	A	Y	Y

Session 8

Coming Home

Objectives

This session has three objectives:

- To help the young people relate the parable of the prodigal son to the experience of forgiveness in their own life
- To invite them to examine where they are in need of forgiveness
- To encourage them to experience the cleansing of sin through the sacrament of Reconciliation

Background on the Session Theme

In the classic story of the prodigal, a son squanders his father's wealth and good will, then returns to the father seeking menial labor to avoid starving. His father welcomes him back with open arms. The brother of the returning son is not as forgiving.

No matter where young people might be in their relationships with others, they can probably relate to one of the characters in the story. Sometimes they may be the one in need of forgiving, another time they may be the one who can offer forgiveness, and often they may be the one holding the grudge. No matter who they identify with at the moment, young people, like us, need to be assured that no matter what happens, they can always come back to God the Father, who awaits them with open arms.

The other Scripture readings highlighted in this session continue this theme of God's compassion and great mercy for us. In the reading from Exodus, God heeds Moses' plea on behalf of the people and forgoes punishing the Israelites who had started to worship false gods. In Psalm 51 the author experiences a shower of God's cleansing forgiveness as mercy wipes away sinfulness.

Schedule at a Glance

Session Activities (Total session time: 90 minutes)

A. **Introduction** (5 minutes)

B. **It's in the Cards** (10 minutes), a large-group icebreaker introducing the topic of forgiveness

C. **The Prodigal Son** (10 minutes), a video sharing the parable of the prodigal son in a different way

D. **The Prodigal Daughter** (20 minutes), a small-group discussion on a contemporary version of the parable

E. **Snack Break** (10 minutes)

F. **The Stain of Sin** (15 minutes), a hands-on activity on the effect of sin and the power of forgiveness in relationships

G. **You Can Always Come Home** (20 minutes), an individual prayer and quiet-time activity

Materials Needed

This is a list of materials needed for all the activities in this session, except the optional activity:

- ☐ Bibles, one for each person
- ☐ a deck of playing cards
- ☐ a television
- ☐ a VCR
- ☐ one of the videos listed in activity C
- ☐ copies of handout 8–A, "The Prodigal Daughter," one for each small group
- ☐ pens or pencils
- ☐ snacks
- ☐ large trash bags, one for each small group
- ☐ newspapers, a large stack for each small group
- ☐ bowls of water, one for each small group

- ☐ small towels, one for each small group
- ☐ copies of handout 8–B, "Responsorial Psalm," one for each person
- ☐ copies of handout 8–C, "The Prodigal Teen," one for each person
- ☐ a basket
- ☐ a pillar candle and matches (optional)

Other Necessary Preparations

- ☐ *For activity C.* Cue the video and check the picture and the volume. If possible, use a big-screen television so that all the young people will be able to see the video from where they sit.
- ☐ *For activity G.* Cut and fold the copies of handout 8–C. If possible, arrange to hold this activity in a chapel or other worship space where the young people can spread out and work separately. If such a room is unavailable, create your own sacred space by lighting a pillar candle and using softer lighting in the room.
- ☐ Review the optional activity at the end of this session and consider whether you would like to use it in some way, for example, in place of another activity, as a way to extend the session, or as a follow-up activity.

Session Activities

Activity A Introduction (5 minutes)

Related Scripture passage. Luke 15:11–32

Materials needed. Bibles, one for each person

1. Distribute Bibles to everyone. Ask the young people if they have ever heard the story of the prodigal son. Talk about how it is one of the most popular parables in the Gospels, probably because most of us can relate to it in one way or another—either as the person who needs forgiveness or as the one who needs to do the forgiving or as the one who holds a grudge.

2. Invite a teen to proclaim Luke 15:11–32. Have the others follow along in their Bible.

Activity B It's in the Cards (10 minutes)

Materials needed. a deck of playing cards

1. Give each teen one playing card. Make sure the suits (hearts, diamonds, clubs, and spades) are distributed evenly. For example, if you have twenty participants, you should give out five heart cards, five diamond cards, five club cards, and five spade cards.

2. Call out the following groupings of cards (and young people) one at a time. After everyone has found a partner or partners, ask one of the discussion questions listed below. Note that if you aren't using a full deck, you may need to eliminate or alter some of the groups suggested below (for example, a four-of-a-kind grouping might not work).

Groupings
- Find someone with the same suit (for example, a heart card pairs up with another heart card).
- Find someone with the same color card as you (for example, a diamond may pair up with a heart; a spade may team up with a club).
- Find someone with a different color suit than you (for example, a spade could pair up with a diamond or a heart).
- Find someone whose card when added to yours creates an even number.
- Find someone whose card when added to yours creates an odd number.
- Find someone with the same number or face card.
- Find three other people whose cards along with your card create four-of-a-kind.
- Find three other people whose cards along with your card represent all four suits.
- Find three other people whose cards along with your card create a straight (for example, 2, 3, 4, and 5)

Questions for discussion
- What is another word for forgiveness?
- Give an example of a time when Jesus forgave someone.
- Why is it hard to forgive others?
- Why is it hard to ask for forgiveness?
- Why is it scary sometimes to go to confession?
- Why do we need to receive the sacrament of Reconciliation?
- How does it feel to know God will always forgive you?
- Why is it hard to let go of a grudge?
- Why do we need to let go of grudges?
- How can we be more forgiving people?

Activity C The Prodigal Son (10 minutes)

Related Scripture passage. Luke 15:11–32

Materials needed. a television, a VCR, one of the following videos:
- *The Prodigal Son* from *God's Trombones: A Trilogy of African American Poems* (Billy Budd Films, 235 East Fifty-seventh Street, New York, NY 10022; phone 212-755-3968)
- *A Father and Two Sons* (American Bible Society, P.O. Box 7251, Berlin, CT 06037; phone 800-322-4253)

Before the session. Make sure a VCR is connected and tuned to the right station. Cue up the video to check the picture and the volume. If possible, use a big-screen television so that all the young people will be able to see the video from where they sit.

1. Introduce this activity in these or similar words:

- The parable of the prodigal son can be told in many ways, and we relive the story again and again in our own life. Tonight we will share with you two other ways of retelling the story—one in video, and the other from a contemporary point of view.

2. Show the video *The Prodigal Son* from *God's Trombones: A Trilogy of African American Poems* or *A Father and Two Sons.* Move immediately into the next activity.

Activity D The Prodigal Daughter (20 minutes)

Related Scripture passage. Luke 15:11–32

Materials needed. copies of handout 8–A, "The Prodigal Daughter," one for each small group; pens or pencils

1. Ask the young people to move into small groups. You may want to use the last grouping from the "It's in the Cards" activity. Distribute handout 8–A, "The Prodigal Daughter," which is an adaptation of the Scripture passage Luke 15:11–32. Ask one person from each group to read the story aloud before the group discusses the questions on the handout.

2. Ask each small group to appoint a spokesperson to share its answers with the large group.

Activity E Snack Break (10 minutes)

Activity F The Stain of Sin (15 minutes)

Related Scripture passage. Psalm 51

Materials needed. large trash bags, one for each small group; newspapers, a large stack for each small group; bowls of water, one for each small group; small towels, one for each small group; copies of handout 8–B, "Responsorial Psalm," one for each person

1. Give each small group one trash bag and a stack of newspapers. Tell the young people that on your signal, they are to crumple the newspapers into balls, one sheet at a time, and stuff them in the bag. Everyone in the group must work together on this task.

2. When the young people are finished, invite each group to get a bowl of water and a towel with which to wash the ink off their hands. Explain that they may not wash their own hands but must each wash the hands of someone else in their small group.

3. When they are finished, distribute handout 8–B, "Responsorial Psalm," and invite the entire group to pray Psalm 51 as a responsorial psalm.

4. Pose the following questions to the large group:
- What did you learn about sin from this activity?
- What did you learn about forgiveness from this activity?
- How might you connect the psalm we just prayed to this activity?

5. Close this activity with these or similar words:
- Peer pressure can be a cause of temptation. Sometimes the stain of sin can touch us before we even realize it. But God always gives us a chance to clean up our act. We seek reconciliation from others as well as from God.

Activity G — You Can Always Come Home (20 minutes)

Related Scripture passages. Exodus 32:7–11,13–14; Luke 15:11–32

Materials needed. copies of handout 8–C, "The Prodigal Teen," one for each person; pens or pencils; a basket; a pillar candle and matches (optional)

Before the session. Cut and fold the copies of handout 8–C, one for each person. If possible, arrange to hold this activity in a chapel or other worship space where the young people can spread out and work separately. If such a room is unavailable, create your own sacred space by lighting a pillar candle and using softer lighting in the room.

1. Introduce the importance of making time for quiet in our life, especially in our often noisy and frenetic everyday life. Invite the young people to take some quiet time now to reflect on and pray the Scriptures of tonight's session.

2. Give each teen a copy of handout 8–C, "The Prodigal Teen," that you prepared before the session. Ask everyone to spread out in your worship space or chapel and work on their own. Direct the young people to reflect on the video and story and reread the Scripture passage on the prodigal son in their Bible. They should then write their own prayer asking forgiveness for a time when they turned away from God.

3. After those who wish to do so have written a prayer, invite them to quietly place it in a basket in front of the Blessed Sacrament. Assure the young people that the prayers will not be read.

Optional Activity — Sinful Words, Caring Words (20 minutes)

Related Scripture passage. 1 Timothy 1:12–17

Materials needed. sixteen index cards, a pen or pencil

Before the session. Write on a separate index card each of the eight sinful or hurtful phrases and eight caring or loving phrases listed below:

Sinful or hurtful phrases	*Caring or loving phrases*
Leave me alone.	I love you.
You can't do it.	Hi, how are you?
Don't bother me.	You did great.
I hate you.	May I help?
I don't care.	You are forgiven.
Get lost.	Thank you.
You are stupid.	You did it!
Go away.	I am sorry.

1. Begin by reading 1 Timothy 1:12–17. Then divide the large group into two teams and give each team four sinful cards and four caring cards. Ask the participants to begin with the sinful or hurtful phrases. Ask one person in the group to draw a card and express or act out the emotion or feeling associated with the phrase until her or his group guesses it. For each one, ask the entire group,
• How does it make you feel when you are treated this way?
Continue this process for all four cards.

2. Repeat the process for the caring or loving words. When they have finished, ask the young people if they can name other sinful or hurting phrases and caring or loving phrases.

3. Close this activity with these or similar words:
• We choose which words we use and which words we avoid. In your relationships with others, you are challenged to choose caring or loving words instead of sinful or hurtful words.
In our reading today from First Timothy, Paul tells us that he was once a blasphemer and a persecutor, but through Christ he turned his life around. If we follow Christ, we too can make the right choices and change the way we treat others and become more forgiving and compassionate people.

Scripture References

Additional Scripture Passages

Psalm 103. God loves us with mercy.
Psalm 130. God forgives our sins.
Exodus 24:4–6,8–9. Moses asks God to forgive the people.
Matthew 18:21–35. Forgive without limit.
Ephesians 2:4–10. God is always merciful.
2 Corinthians 5:17–21. Christ reconciles the world.

Lectionary Readings

Cycle A
Twenty-fourth Sunday of Ordinary Time

Cycle B
Seventh Sunday of Ordinary Time

Cycle C
Fourth Sunday of Lent
Seventh Sunday of Ordinary Time
Eleventh Sunday of Ordinary Time
Twenty-fourth Sunday of Ordinary Time

Session Follow-Up

Family Connection

Suggest to the young people that they try the following activity at home. Make copies of the directions to send home with them. If your parish will be having a reconciliation service soon, send an invitation for the family to attend as a group rather than have the young people attend and sit as a class.

> Read aloud the story of the prodigal son, Luke 15:11–32. Then begin a dialogue on the need for forgiveness by inviting each person to choose and complete one of the following sentence starters:
> - Sometimes I feel like the father when . . .
> - Sometimes I feel like the prodigal son when . . .
> - Sometimes I feel like the other brother when . . .

The Prodigal Daughter

Once upon a time, there was a single mother living with her daughter and son. They were a close and happy family, and they got along for the most part, although they did fight now and then.

One day, after the daughter had graduated from high school, she went to her mother and said, "I am eighteen and old enough to be on my own. Please give me all the money we have saved up for my college tuition. I want to travel and see the world, get a job, and start living in a new and exciting place."

The mother was sad. She tried to convince her daughter to stay home with the family and go to a local college, but the daughter refused. So the mother gave her the money and said good-bye.

The daughter went to a big city and rented an apartment. She made a lot of friends and went out to eat every night. She was having so much fun that she kept forgetting to look for a job. Eventually, she ran out of money, and she was kicked out of her apartment. The daughter found out that getting a job isn't easy. So she just walked the streets, eating whatever food she could find in the dumpsters behind the restaurants where she used to be a customer. And nobody seemed to recognize her, and no one wanted to help her.

The daughter finally decided to go back home and ask her mother to hire her as a housekeeper. She figured she could cook, clean, and take care of the house, because she could never return home as a real daughter—not after wasting all that money.

So the daughter returned home. Her mother was so happy to see her that she threw her arms around her and kissed her dirty face, brought her in, and poured her a cup of hot chocolate. The mother called for her son to come downstairs and celebrate. Then she called all her friends and relatives and told them to come over right away because her daughter had come back.

The daughter could not believe all this attention! She got hugs and kisses and presents from all her aunts and uncles and cousins whom she hadn't seen for a long time.

Eventually, the mother realized that her son had not come downstairs from his bedroom. She went up to get him.

The son was furious. He started screaming at his mother so loudly that everyone downstairs heard him: "How could you do this? How could you reward her after she wasted all the money you saved up for her college education? She never even got a job! Look at her! She's a mess! I am embarrassed to be her brother. I've been here all along; I get the good grades; I have a part-time job; I help around the house, and you never gave me a party! That's why I'm not coming down to her stupid party."

The mother pleaded with him. "You are my only son, and I have enjoyed living with you all of these years. You are wonderful, and I am so thankful that you have been with me. But no matter how angry you are at your sister, she is still your sister. And even if she used up all her money, she is still alive! It's been so long since we have seen her, I thought she was dead! So I'm so excited that she's back. You haven't even said hello to her. Please come downstairs and join us."

How Does This Story End?

A. The son refuses to come down and join the party, so the daughter finally goes upstairs. She knocks on the bedroom door, and he says, "Come in." Then what happens?

B. The son goes downstairs, and when he sees his sister, he remembers how much he loves her, so he goes over to talk to her. Then what happens?

C. The son himself decides to leave. He packs his bags, and on his way out the back door, his sister sees him and calls out his name. He turns around and sees her for the first time since she came home. Then what happens?

Questions for Discussion

1. Pick your favorite ending.
2. Decide what happens next. What does the brother say and do? What does the sister say and do? What does the mother say and do?
3. How does this story relate to the video you just saw? How is the mother like God? How are we sometimes like the prodigal daughter?
4. What are some of the things we say and do that are in need of forgiveness?

(This story is from Lisa-Marie Calderone-Stewart, *FaithWorks for Junior High,* pages 70–71.)

Responsorial Psalm

I will rise and go to my father.

Have mercy on me, O God,
according to your steadfast love;
according to your abundant mercy
blot out my transgressions.
Wash me thoroughly from my iniquity,
and cleanse me from my sin.
(Verses 1–2)

Response. I will rise and go to my father.

Create in me a clean heart, O God,
and put a new and right spirit within me.
Do not cast me away from your presence,
and do not take your holy spirit from me.
(Verses 10–11)

Response. I will rise and go to my father.

O Lord, open my lips,
and my mouth will declare your praise. . . .
The sacrifice acceptable to God is a broken spirit;
a broken and contrite heart, O God, you will not despise.
(Psalm 51:15–17)

Response. I will rise and go to my father.

The Prodigal Teen

Act of Contrition (Prayer of Sorrow)

O my God, I am sorry for my sins. In failing to do good, I have sinned against you, and your church. I firmly promise, with the help of your Son, to make up for my sins, and share your peace.
Amen.

Dear God,
Please forgive me for . . .

____

____

____

____

____

____

The Prodigal Teen

Luke 15:11–32

What the Scriptures Say . . . and Don't Say: Reading the Bible in Context

by
Margaret Nutting Ralph

Have you ever heard two people who totally disagree with each other use Scripture to "prove" that God is on their side? Instead of letting the Scriptures form their thinking, they use a quote from the Scriptures, often taken out of context, to support their own opinions.

We've probably all done this to some extent. Even expert theologians use Scripture quotes to show that their teaching is rooted in the Bible. But a proper understanding of biblical revelation will challenge us to examine our approach to the Scriptures and overcome any tendency to quote the Bible out of context.

Instead of asking, "Do these words support what I already think?" we need to ask, "What is this passage trying to teach me?" When we recognize what the inspired biblical authors intended to teach, we are opening our minds and hearts to the revelation of the Scriptures.

The revealed Scriptures do not necessarily hold the same meaning we may want to attach to the words. The inspired biblical authors intended to say and teach certain truths, and we need to root our understanding of the Scriptures first and foremost in the intent of the author.

But how do we determine the intentions of an author who lived thousands of years ago in a totally different cultural setting? The church teaches us that in order to understand the revelation the Bible contains, we must learn first and foremost to read passages in the context in which they appear.

What are you reading? One way to safeguard against misunderstanding the intent of an author is to determine the kind of writing the author has chosen to use. Any piece of writing has a particular literary form: poetry, prose, fiction, essay, letter, historical account, and so on. This is as true of the biblical books as of any piece of contemporary writing.

If we misunderstand an author's literary form, we will misunderstand what the author intends to say. In order to understand what we are reading, then, we have to make allowances for the form and change our expectations accordingly.

We do this any time we read a newspaper, for example. As we turn the pages of a newspaper, we encounter a variety of literary forms—news, features, editorials, and so on—and we adjust our idea of what we can expect from the writing for each form.

For instance, after I read a news story, I expect to have the answer to the question What happened? I expect the author of a news story to be objective and evenhanded, to inform me of the facts. If the story is about something controversial, I expect the writer to cover all sides fairly.

When I get to the editorial page, I change my expectations. Now I know that the author is allowed to be persuasive rather than objective. I may find facts that support the author's point of view but nothing that contradicts that point of view.

So if I read an editorial with the same frame of mind with which I read a front-page news story, thinking that the author has responded to the question What happened?, I will be misinformed after I finish my reading. It is not the author's fault that I am misinformed. It is my own.

How the inspired author tells the tale. Now lets look at how literary form functions in the Bible. One of the inspired biblical authors—the author of the Book of Job—has written in the form of a debate. This literary form demands that you be as persuasive as possible on both sides of an issue. If you write persuasively on the side you agree with and poorly on the side you disagree with, you have not written a good debate.

The author of the Book of Job lived at a time when people believed that all suffering was punishment for sin. He wrote a debate to argue against this belief. The author places his debate in the context of a preexisting legend that establishes at the outset the fact that Job is innocent. So why is he suffering?

The author portrays Job's friends arguing with Job over the cause of his suffering. All the friends think that Job must have sinned or he wouldn't be suffering. They do not know, as does the audience, that Job's sinfulness is not the source of his suffering. The friends are wrong.

Now, if you did not know that the Book of Job is a debate, in which some of the characters argue persuasively for the point of view with which the author disagrees, you might read an isolated passage and conclude that the book teaches the opposite of what the author intended to teach. You might think that the friends are teaching a valid message about suffering.

If we look at the book as a whole, we discover that the author places the truth he is teaching not on the lips of Job's friends but on the lips of God. God appears at the end of the debate and responds to the friends' arguments. Obviously, the author agrees with what God has to say. God contradicts the belief that all suffering is punishment for sin.

Because this book is in the canon, we know that it teaches revealed truth. We can only discover this revealed truth, however, if we look at the literary form of the book.

We need to remember, too, that the Bible is actually a "library" of many different books. To say that Job is a debate is not to say that the Bible as a whole is a debate or that a Gospel is a debate or that the Book of Revelation is a debate. The answer to the question What literary form am I reading? will vary from book to book. Often the introduction to each book in a good study Bible will give you the relevant literary form.

Culture in context. We have seen how easy it is to "misquote" the Bible by taking passages out of the context of their literary form. A second context we need to consider is the culture and the beliefs in place when the book was written. The inspired author and the original audience shared knowledge, presumptions, expressions, and concerns that may not be part of our awareness, but may nevertheless influence the meaning of the book or passage.

The inspired author may have applied the revealed message contained in a particular book to a shared cultural setting in order to make the message clearer. People sometimes mistake such applications for the heart of the revealed message. Thus they put the full authority of the Scriptures behind passages that reflect beliefs of the time rather than the unchanging truth the author intended to teach.

In expressing the revealed truth, a biblical author may show cultural biases and presumptions that later generations know are inaccurate. This kind of misunderstanding resulted in Galileo's excommunication. We know, as biblical authors did not, that the earth is not the center of the universe or even our solar system. We also know that the Bible does not claim to teach astronomy. Rather, the Bible addresses questions about the relationship between God and God's people, about what we should be doing to build up God's Kingdom rather than to tear it down.

A biblical author may also apply an eternal truth to a setting that is important to the original audience but not to us. For example, one of Paul's key insights is that the way we treat every other person is the way we treat the risen Christ. He applies this insight to the social order of his own day, an order that included slavery. We misuse the Scriptures if we say this application shows that *God's* social order includes slavery. While Paul's core message is eternally true revelation, the application was relevant only in its own cultural context.

Revelation is ongoing. A third context we must be aware of is the place the inspired author's insights have in the process of revelation. The Bible is not a book of bottom-line answers like a catechism.

The Bible is a "library of books" written over a two-thousand-year period. It reflects the process by which the inspired authors came to greater knowledge of God's revealed truth. People who do not realize or do not believe that the Bible reflects this progression take an early insight as the whole truth.

For example, people may make this mistake when arguing over the death penalty. Some people who support the death penalty try to put God's authority behind their opinion by quoting Scripture: An eye for an eye, a tooth for a tooth, a life for a life.

It is true that the Scriptures teach this (see Ex. 21:23–24). However, the teaching dates to the time of Exodus, about 1250 B.C.E. At the time, this teaching was an ethical step forward. It taught people not to seek escalating revenge: If you harm me, I can't do worse to you than you originally did to me.

Jesus later challenged people to grow beyond this teaching. He said, "You have heard that it was said, 'an eye for an eye and a tooth for a tooth. . . .' But I say to you, Love your enemies and pray for those who persecute you" (Matthew 5:38–44). Jesus did not say that the law was wrong, only that it did not go far enough. Jesus is the fulfillment of the law.

We are misusing the Scriptures if we quote Exodus to support the death penalty and fail to quote the words of Jesus in the Gospels. When we use a passage from the Scriptures to support our side of an argument, we must ask ourselves if the passage reflects the fullness of truth or whether it is a partial truth, perhaps an early insight.

Context, context, context. It is distressing to hear Christians abuse the Bible by quoting it in favor of unchristian positions. It is doubly distressing to realize that we ourselves might be guilty of this.

One way to avoid this mistake is to remember always to consider the context. Determine the place of a passage in its larger context. Ask yourself what literary form the author is using. Explore the beliefs and presumptions the author may share with the original audience. Learn something about the time when the book was written. Know how the author's insights fit into the process of revelation.

If we do this, we will avoid many a harmful error. We will be less likely to abuse the Scriptures and more likely to hear the revelation of God's love that the biblical authors intend us to hear.

Finally, invite the Holy Spirit to open up your mind and heart as you listen to the word. Discerning God's will in your life will leave you with Christ's own peace in your heart.

Margaret Nutting Ralph is secretary for educational ministries for the Diocese of Lexington, Kentucky, and director of the master's degree programs for Roman Catholics at Lexington Theological Seminary. She has taught the Scriptures to high school students, college students, and adult education groups for twenty years. She is the author of the book and video *And God Said What?* and the Discovering the Living Word series (all from Paulist Press).

Guidelines for Small-Group Leaders

1. Familiarize yourself with the session so that you will be better prepared to give directions and process activities.
2. Prepare and organize your supplies.
3. Participate in all games, prayers, and discussions with the young people.
4. Lead, encourage, affirm, support, and befriend the participants.
5. Help the participants feel welcome and comfortable.
6. Help each person in the group get to know the others better.
7. Be aware of the shy persons (who need more encouragement) and the rowdy ones (who need some calming down). Learn about the young peoples' lives outside your meeting or class so that you can better understand what they are dealing with in school and at home.
8. Help the participants keep to a given topic and guide the discussion.
9. Never tell the participants what they have learned. Instead draw the answers from their sharing.
10. Contribute to, but do not dominate, the discussion. Do not feel as though you have to fill in any quiet gaps.
11. If you have trouble getting a discussion started, vary how you decide who will begin the sharing. For example, start with the person who has the most letters on his or her shirt, has the next birthday, has the longest name, has the highest house number in his or her street address, and so on.
12. Ask open-ended questions:
    - How do you feel?
    - What is your reaction?
    - What do you think?
    - What would you do in this situation?
    - What would Jesus do?
13. Make sure everyone is included, that everyone participates and has a chance to voice their opinion. Stress that each person's contribution is valuable.